Newsthinking

Newsthinking

The Secret of Making Your Facts Fall into Place

Bob Baker

Los Angeles Times Deputy Metropolitan Editor and Writing Coach

Allyn and Bacon

Boston ■ London ■ Toronto ■ Sydney ■ Tokyo ■ Singapore

Series Editor: Molly Taylor
Editorial Assistant: Sarah McGaughey
Marketing Manager: Jacqueline Aaron
Editorial–Production Service: Matrix Productions Inc.
Composition and Prepress Buyer: Linda Cox
Manufacturing Buyer: Julie McNeill
Cover Administrator: Kristina Mose-Libon
Electronic Composition: Cabot Computer Services

Between the time Website information is gathered and then published, it is not
unusual for some sites to have closed. Also, the transcription of URLs can result
in unintended typographical errors. The publisher would appreciate notification
where these occur so that they may be corrected in subsequent editions.

Library of Congress Cataloging-in-Publication Data

Baker, Bob
    Newsthinking : the secret of making your facts fall into place / by Bob Baker.
      p. cm.
    Includes bibliographical references.
    ISBN 0-321-08756-9
      1. Journalism—Authorship—Psychological aspects. 2. Report writing—
Psychological aspects. I. Title.

PN4781 .B26 2002
808'.06607—dc21   2001022154

The credits appear on page 175, which constitutes a continuation of the
copyright page.

Printed in the United States of America

10 9 8 7 6 5 4 3 2 1   06 05 04 03 02 01

For Marjorie and Amanda

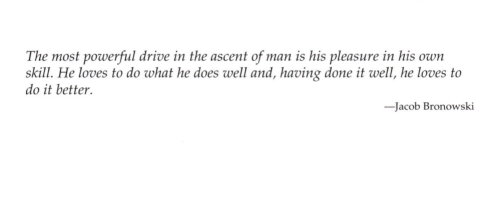

The most powerful drive in the ascent of man is his pleasure in his own skill. He loves to do what he does well and, having done it well, he loves to do it better.

—Jacob Bronowski

. . . be warned of the good advice of others. Be warned when they tell you that your attitude is immature. Be warned against all "good" advice because "good" advice is necessarily "safe" advice, and though it will undoubtedly follow a sane pattern, it will very likely lead one into total sterility—one of the crushing problems of our time.

—Jules Feiffer

CONTENTS

FOREWORD

I first met Bob Baker through a book. This book.

When I became a writing coach at *The Oregonian* in 1988, I soon realized that most newswriting problems went deeper than choosing the right verb or knowing the difference between a simile and an allusion. Stories wandered off in all directions because they lacked a strong focus inherent in the original idea. They left loose ends and missed important angles because of poorly planned reporting. They repeated material or confused readers with bad sequencing because reporters didn't bother to organize their notes. I began to realize, in short, that what you do before you put your hands on the keyboard determines what you do when you put your hands on the keyboard.

So I started looking for a book that would help writers realize the importance of crafting the right kind of ideas, planning their reporting, and organizing their material. Nothing.

I'd nearly given up when I found *Newsthinking*. It is, I believe, the first prewriting book written from a journalistic perspective. It was a breakthrough in the way journalists thought about their craft. It was also out of print; Writer's Digest Books had published only 10,000 copies. So that's how I met Bob. I called him at the *Los Angeles Times* and found out that he still had some copies of *Newsthinking* stashed in his garage. I ordered two for our newsroom library.

Bob and I talked on the phone several times after that, and eventually we met face-to-face. Now we check in with each other on a regular basis.

Over those years one of *The Oregonian*'s library copies of *Newsthinking* has disappeared, the victim of some reporter who apparently found it too valuable to return. But we still have the other, and it remains one of the most important books in the short list I recommend to reporters regularly.

But books disappear easily in newsrooms, and someday somebody will snatch our last copy of *Newsthinking*. That certain knowledge is one reason I'm so happy that Bob has decided to make the manuscript available again. I plan to be the first customer for the new edition.

One of the things that makes *Newsthinking* so valuable is that it's an example of a reporter talking to other reporters. Bob came by his hard-won knowledge first-hand during eleven years at the *L.A. Times* on a variety of news and feature beats. He has a lot of credibility with other reporters, who tend to distrust the ivory-tower opinions of editors and writing coaches.

But Bob's seen journalism from the editing side, too. He was city editor at the Thousand Oaks, California, *News-Chronicle* and has served for twelve years as an editor and writing coach at the *L.A. Times,* where he's currently a deputy metropolitan editor.

That's important experience, too. Most writers assume that other writers work in pretty much the same way they do. But editors know better. They quickly experience the wide variety of abilities that characterize reporting and writing in any newsroom, and they have a perspective that allows them to see the importance of prewriting.

If only they will.

In years past, most newsrooms operated like Henry Ford's assembly line: Copy passed from hand to hand until it finally ended up on somebody's doorstep. Reporters often received their assignments from one editor, worked on the reporting and writing in isolation, and turned the finished draft in to yet another editor. Not surprisingly, the editor on the receiving end seldom looked past the copy he or she had just been handed. Prewriting was a vague notion that seldom, if ever, received any attention.

Boy, have things changed. Now we're disciples of the notion that quality should be built into the front end, rather than inspected into the back end. The world of journalism, in other words, has discovered the writing process. Writing conferences, sessions at the Poynter Institute, and the American Press Institute, and coaching newsletters all spend an increasing amount of time preaching prewriting. The current crop of writing gurus has divided the process a little more finely than Bob did. And they've cogitated deeply about the various routines that will help reporters work their way through each step of the process. But none of them has challenged the basic idea that *Newsthinking* represented.

So every year I realize a little more about the depth of Bob's insight when he conceived the theme of *Newsthinking* in 1978. He saw then what most of us are only beginning to realize now. And he explored some dimensions of prewriting—particularly when it comes to the creative, right-brain kinds of things that can occur during prewriting—that others have yet to tackle.

Newsthinking was a book published before its time, and it remains a good and worthwhile read despite the fact that it was first published in 1981. If you missed it the first time around, I commend it to you now. After all, most of us are just reaching the point at which we can truly appreciate it.

Jack Hart
Managing Editor/Weekends
The Oregonian

PREFACE

I hated it. A reporter would break his neck for hours or days, come up with first-class information, and then write a second-class story. A piece that missed the point or was far too wordy or just didn't live up to its potential. He or she would romp into the city room, gleefully bellowing the juicy details, sit down at the typewriter, and an hour or two later I'd be reading the copy, shaking my head and asking myself, "What was all the fuss about?"

Of all the frustrations I encountered as a rookie editor, that kind of disappointment was the worst. "You didn't *think!*" I'd complain. But the reporter could just as easily have shot back, "What the hell do you mean, exactly?"

I hope this book is the answer. I hope it teaches you how to think when you write a story.

This book is devoted to improving the prewriting process—the thought process all reporters go through before they hit the first key. It is an intense examination of those moments in which you make your facts fall into place. This is *newsthinking*, in which the genius of great writers—their creativity, their imagination, their willingness to take risks—unfolds. Much of it is subconscious, but most of it is also structured. The reporter or book author or magazine essayist you admire may appear to be an artist whose impulses arise from a deep, mysterious font, but in fact this mastery is produced in a laboratory. With the sophistication of a scientist, the writer has built and refined a complex set of thought strategies, a system in which nothing is left to chance, in which each sentence and paragraph is automatically and rigorously tested.

He knows that writing is not merely an aesthetic ballet in which words dance onto paper. Writing is thinking.

All good writers understand this, but they also know that the process is an intensely personal one built on layer after layer of habits so deeply ingrained and complex that they defy simple description. How can any writer tell you, in five or ten minutes, how to think through a story? As a result, many reporters—especially the successful ones—adopt the pose of artist rather than mechanic, and it's hard to blame them. After all, we merely admire proficient mechanics; we marvel at artists.

The goal of this book is the same in 2001 as it was when it was first published twenty years ago: to cut through that facade by revealing to you the thought processes and mental attitudes a highly skilled reporter uses to sort through thousands of facts and organize them into literate, perceptive, and creative copy. Whether your goal is to write newspaper stories or novels or biographies or publicity releases for a community organization, you will profit by building that same sort of system for yourself.

Newsthinking, the inner game of newswriting, is a marvelous performance, a testament to the human brain's capacity—and yet it is almost never analyzed. It is one of those achievements regarded as natural by those reporters who write well and as magic by those who can't.

Whom should we believe? Both sides sound logical: Newswriting is natural, a blend of hundreds of mental and physical steps ordered and monitored by the brain. And it's magic—at least, when you're working at the peak of your game and the words are flowing and the creative impulses are coming out of nowhere and the story writes itself, it seems like magic, right?

Forget it. If you want to keep thinking like that, you're settling for less. You're squandering your talent. You're taking the easy way out. Because writing, although one of the most complex mental and social acts a human can perform, is nevertheless a definable skill like any other. You improve it by making more efficient use of your inherited attributes. The people who best succeed at increasing their efficiency are those who concentrate the hardest on doing so.

Sadly, among most reporters and editors there is little emphasis on either concentration or improvement of writing—and it shows. The quality of writing in the average newspaper remains woeful. It discourages potential readers from delving more deeply into the news and it discourages people with first-rate minds from devoting themselves to news work. They burn out or grow disenchanted too quickly.

To avoid getting caught in that quagmire, you have to begin looking at the world of newswriting in a different way. You have to stop concentrating on merely the results of good writing—the examples they show you in most textbooks. You have to begin thinking about the causes—the thought strategies that created those polished samples.

To do that, you need a massive injection of vision and imagination. Because the only way to improve your prewriting process—your ability to organize information and make the right choices—is to look inside yourself, to look hard at what you're doing. There is no physical evidence here, no scrapbook of story clippings; instead, you must visualize the stages of mental preparation you now go through, and then begin bolstering them. You must build them into a more thorough, more efficient information-processing system.

Even the least skilled reporter works according to some kind of subconscious mental formula, some crude, unspoken plan by which he decides how to conduct an interview, what questions to ask, when to take notes, how to use his memory, test his creativity, write his leads. The trouble is, this unskilled reporter has no idea that his mental processes are shallow because he seldom talks to another reporter about the inner game. He rarely compares, so he rarely learns.

But we will. We will show you, for one thing, that the mental development of any story—news, feature, obituary, whatever—follows a general chain of thought. Some of the steps in this cycle of information processing may seem obvious to you, but what's more important is the unity among them. The steps—we have nine elemental ones—are an obstacle course that no one ever runs perfectly or without variation. What's so enticing about writing is finding out how close to perfection you can come. As you study the steps, you'll realize that you, and most other working newsmen and women, are far, far away from your optimum level.

By the time you finish this book, you should be building your skills with goals far higher than those of the average journalist. You should never again have to worry about competing against another reporter, because there will be a new, more challenging target to take aim at: your own potential.

This book is not a miracle cure. It assumes you have or will acquire sound news instincts and a passion for newswriting. Without them, you may build an elaborate, polished mental system but you'll still crank out nothing but well-structured oatmeal. You may turn out to be just what the "happy news" television consultants want, but you won't be a good reporter.

This book wouldn't be needed if so many newspapers—and so many of their reporters—weren't so willing to settle for so little. Pick up any newspaper and examples abound. There's the feature story that was blown because the writer didn't use his heart. The news story with the real news in the ninth paragraph because the writer didn't have the guts to depart from the chronology and define the essence of what he observed. The half-hearted analysis of a local water district audit, so thickly littered with uninterpreted financial details that only an accountant—not the average reader who deals with the district only when paying the bill—could understand it.

Spread the blame all you want to (the way they don't teach writing in high school any more, the way newspaper staffs are kept too thin, there are a dozen more excuses if you'd like to fill them in here). But the spotlight inevitably falls on the reporter. He wrote those stories; he blew them. He had the control. He had the power. He had the facts. And he had the keyboard. What went wrong was inside his head, and if we want to improve the quality of newswriting, we have to start there.

Acknowledgments

For their advice, encouragement, and inspiration, thanks to Lillian, Earl, and Alan Baker, Russ Barnard, Nigel Calder, Carol Cartaino, Mary Curtius,

INTRODUCTION

Take a few minutes. Look around your classroom or newsroom and find the best writer. Watch her type. Why is she better? Why, if all of you collected the same information before writing a story, would hers be the one that an editor would run?

The answer lies in the brain or, if you wish to use a broader term, in the mind. That skilled reporter's brain has organized the thinking and writing process into a highly efficient series of steps—a far more refined process than the one you use. From there, her brain has learned that basic structure so well that many of the steps begin to come in clusters—she doesn't have to worry about performing them one step at a time.

Remember, we are not talking about her physical capacity; you don't increase the number of muscle fibers in your arms when you do three sets of ten curls a night, you merely increase the strength and endurance of your existing muscles. In the same way, that reporter has developed her ability to organize a story not by increasing the number of active nerve cells in her brain (adults can't do that), but by improving the extent and subtlety of the nerve cells' interconnections and their readiness to fire.

That's not magic. But that's why she appears to have a "quick mind," to jump several thoughts ahead in crucial situations. Her brain has learned to combine a series of steps in this basic composition process without having to monitor the feedback step by step. That's what allows her, for example, to read through a budget and quickly glean the correct lead, while you move more slowly, not as sure of what you're looking for, lacking that sense of structure between each thought.

That's why she can put more thought into her story than you can, and why she can do it in less time. That's why her stories always feature good transitions between paragraphs, while yours keep being rewritten. That's why her stories always seem to provide the correct perspective on an event, while the copy desk has to do so much inserting in yours. That's why her leads are always crisp and never butchered by the desk. That's why her features are usually bright and creative, as though a separate voice—not the usual bang-bang-bang, hard-news voice—were composing them.

Now, when we walk across the room to ask this reporter to explain how she does all this, we run into an eighteenth-century German philosopher: "When the psychical powers are in action," Immanuel Kant says, "one does not observe oneself, and when one observes oneself, those powers stop. A person noticing that someone is watching him and is trying to explore him will either become embarrassed, in which case he *cannot* show himself as he is; or he will disguise himself, in which case he does not *want* to be recognized for what he is."

And so by the time we finish asking that reporter just how it's done, she is ready with answers like, "I dunno, it's just there," or "Some days, it's just hittin'," or "I never know what I think until I see it on paper."

What you're hearing is, "It's magic. I have it, you don't. Tough luck." We're back to where we started. It's this attitude—even when voiced kindly—that explains why some very good reporters turn out to be mediocre editors: They can't teach because they have never understood their own processes.

Remember, even magic has structure. Since World War II, psychologists and engineers have been studying human skills, examining assembly-line workers, executives, and athletes in an attempt to answer the misleadingly simple question "How does he *do* it?" In each area, they have tried to break down the broad components of a skill that had been largely taken for granted, trying to explain how the brain issues commands to the body and then regulates the action. They have learned the basic techniques humans use to achieve skilled performance.

One of the most significant conclusions derived from studies of complex industrial processing operations is that the skilled operator appears to build a "conceptual framework" or model of the mental and physical processes he is using and the manner in which they function. He uses his imagination to construct a mental picture of the way he does his job. Often, he can't put it into words without a tremendous amount of effort, but that doesn't bother him. All he wants is a standard—a sense of how it should *feel* to do the job the right way, whether it's running a loading dock, assembling part of a jet plane wing or sorting mail for a Post Office route.

And that's what we're after here: to make you come to grips with your skill, to force you to build and then streamline a model of your writing process, to make you conscious of the need to program your reporter's mind the same way a computer is programmed.

Your central task is the creation of a series of mental filters, one for each step in your prewriting process. Each time you prepare a story, each decision—each rough outline, each question, each piece of information, each new combination of paragraphs—will be run through several or all of the filters. Depending on how proficient you become, this review may take seconds or long, painful minutes. But it is the only way to aim for greatness. Your filters are your standards, tests of completeness which each fact and impulse must undergo. The order in which you subject your facts to your filters is yours to choose; it is an intimate, personal test. So are the kinds of filters you decide to create. The ones described in the following chapters represent a good starting point, but don't be afraid to augment or change them. What's important is to begin formally developing this kind of process, to experience it, to examine it, to know what it feels like when you're working at full blast, and to know when you're off, when your system needs to be strengthened—when the sophistication of that computer program inside your head has to be increased.

As the process of subconsciously routing each story through your filters and monitoring the results becomes more automatic, you can begin taking more risks: You can vary your styles of writing, experiment with structure, cram unusual amounts of information into a particular paragraph—all with the confidence that your chain of filters will test the experiment and reject it if it doesn't work.

Remember the battlefield: Newspaper writing is not "Writing" any more than shooting a basketball at your front-yard hoop is like playing in a basketball game with nine others or strumming a guitar is like playing in a band in front of three thousand people. "Writer" connotes the sun, reflecting on the forces around it. The reality of "newswriter" is the asteroid, being tugged at violently from every angle—sources, bitchy competitors, bitchy editors, bitchy readers, deadlines, space limitations, and the emotional fragility those pressures create.

You may love it, but that's not enough. You have to consciously define your skills by these pressures. You have to examine your talents and build them with the goal of bringing order out of chaos. Newsrooms may offer the quiet of computerized type systems and the coolness of air conditioning, but mentally the craft remains etched in noise and sweat and the millions of pieces of news and non-news that have to be handled. Conquer them or they will kill you.

Your newsthinking must be tailored to the reality of news. Your system of newswriting values has to enable you to continually make aggressive choices about the raw data you confront; to throw out bad (useless) information; to keep the good and process it through your filters, and to invoke rules of flexibility to retrieve any bad information, should the circumstances of the news story change.

This is the kind of system that heightens the unity between your newswriting skills and your brain's natural talent for making rapid-fire choices and double-checking the results. It is the kind of system that merges your discipline and creativity, helping them both to function at the richest level.

With this writing process, you judge each piece of information as soon as it arrives: "Does it belong in my story?" you demand to know, the same way your brain and nervous system constantly screen out useless data that would otherwise bombard your senses. The information that qualifies for your story is analyzed and combined by passing through the filters. Choices are continually being made, in much the same way that your brain initiates, monitors, and regulates behavior through "yes" and "no" impulses fired by its nerve cells.

Does that sound cold? Does it sound like somebody is thinking about hooking electrodes from your frontal lobes to a video display terminal? Not at all. Your brain is your life. You and your writing are an extension of it. It contains an amazing wealth of power, logic, efficiency, and creativity, and the known scope of its resources is growing furiously as neurology and psychology begin to merge.

In the words of British journalist Nigel Calder, contemporary brain research is like sixteenth-century astronomy: "We are the privileged onlookers in a Copernican phase when men are putting their conscious experience into orbit around the brain. We may be waiting for the Isaac Newton of the nervous system who will reveal what holds this (mental) universe together."

Even in a profession as finite as ours, you have a stake in such a lofty perspective. New discoveries by brain and mind researchers have helped us to define the structure of our magic and our potential to improve it. Not long ago, a kind of cult built up around the study of the right hemisphere of the brain. You have two cerebral hemispheres, often performing widely different functions. The left side handles speech and numbers and perceives the world strictly by the chronology in which events happen. The right side is holistic—it expresses itself by nonverbal, subjective, intuitive impulses and allows you to understand relationships between parts and wholes.

Applied to newswriting, the popular right-hemisphere theory maintains that when a reporter writes a good feature story, she uses the right half of her brain to develop a creative angle. She then shifts to her left hemisphere, using it to convert that angle into words and analyze the results, then moves back to the right side for further inspiration, then back to the left side to check it out, and so on.

Is that what really happens in your brain? Can you control it? Scientific opinion is mixed, but the separate talents of the dual hemispheres are clear—the potential is there. Why wait for science to catch up if *envisioning* that kind of back-and-forth process between your logical and emotional sides helps you write better features?

That's the cutting edge: The more clearly you perceive the way your mind collects, shuffles, reshuffles, retrieves, and then spits out the components of your stories, the more you'll write with perspective, authority, and speed. You'll do it because you'll feel, subtly, the chaotic flood of ideas narrowing into a line of thought that will suddenly race from your head to your fingers and produce the story. You'll know something about why it happens, and you'll know something about how to make it happen more often.

The chapters that follow are organized by their importance in the prewriting process and not necessarily by the sequence in which you will use them. Part of the agony and wonderment of newswriting is that nobody can predict the order in which these steps will come into play. It differs every time you start working on a new story.

Each individual's strengths and weaknesses will dictate which stages he needs to concentrate on more. Some reporters who have had trouble writing feature stories may ultimately find the creativity filter their most important one. Others may rely most heavily on the self-editing filter, which is aimed at improving your copy once it's written. But these are refinements, and they cannot be fully exploited without the primary building blocks.

Briefly, here's where we're going: Chapter 1 examines how to develop the arrogant stance needed when you begin sifting information. Next come two chapters on fundamental thought strategies that come into play as you move closer to typing: Chapter 2 illustrates the construction of a mental filter to test your lead paragraphs. Chapter 3 deals with the development of a sequencing filter, which will monitor whether all of the story's facts have been put in proper sequence.

From there, we will concentrate on supplemental filters that will force you to continually ask yourself whether you have made the story relevant to the reader (Chapter 4); whether you have supplied the proper factual perspective (Chapter 5); whether you have made good use of your inner voice in composing the story (Chapter 6); whether you have pushed your creative resources hard enough (Chapters 7 and 8); and whether you have remembered to edit your own copy carefully (Chapter 9). Finally, in Chapter 10, we'll discuss the impact of pressure—an ever-present enemy in newsrooms—on your work.

At the end of most chapters, you'll be referred to specific parts of the book's Appendix. The Appendix consists of excerpts from a *Los Angeles Times* monthly newsletter on writing, "Nuts & Bolts," that I created and have edited since 1998. The excerpts are examples of good and bad writing techniques, primarily from my newspaper, along with a number of insightful essays on specific techniques by my colleagues. Moving from the end of one chapter to the relevant Appendix entries gives you a taste of real-world journalism. Or, you can save the Appendix for one full meal at the end of the book.

Before we begin, however, a bit of guidance:

Rule Number 1: There Are No Rules.

If you remember nothing else, remember Rule Number 1. It is a joyful tribute to the fact that no two news stories or circumstances are the same, that each reporter has to make his own decisions, has to be in control of his own story. When talented people work together, they eventually wind up throwing out all policies except Rule Number 1.

News operations that disregard this rule take on the collective mentality of the golfing gorilla: A man approaches the first tee and sees his friend is waiting with his clubs—and a gorilla. The gorilla plays golf, he explains, putting a driver in the animal's hands and positioning it. The gorilla swings and hits a perfect shot, 210 yards down the fairway. The ball stops fifteen feet from the hole. When the party arrives for the second shot, the man hands the gorilla a putter. The gorilla swings and hits the ball 210 yards again.

The gorilla's human counterpart is the reporter who does a heart-wrenching, two-hour interview with a family whose child is battling a fatal illness, then comes back to the office and writes twelve inches of copy because two days ago the assistant city editor told him his piece on a fund-raising event was too long.

Rule Number 1 makes it clear that if any rules or policies have to exist, they can be broken, crushed whenever the news requires it. The business is too unpredictable for anyone to say "I will *never*. . . ." Rule Number 1 symbolizes the kind of thinking that keeps newspapers vibrant, living entities. It stands flatly against the breed of publishers and editors who use words like "product" to describe what they put out.

Use that rule while you read this book. Some of its ideas will work for you. Some may trigger new insights. Others may fall flat. Please, don't be too rigid. Don't simply accept one author's description of the way a newswriter's mental system works or feels. Building a conceptual framework of your own process is an asset only if it comes from your soul. Your kind of mental filters may feel completely different from mine. You may visualize their operation as doggy doors or windows, through which your stories are processed in the forms of poodles or flies. No matter. Does it help? Then do it.

For the most uninhibited approach to improving the efficiency of your reporter's mind, remember this: There is no consensus in the scientific community about what's going on "up there." Psychologists, neurologists, physiologists—their fields are still separated by generations of rivalry and disparate terminology. And even within each specialty, experts continue to promote competing theories. So you needn't worry about conforming to any doctrines in building a conceptual model of your writing process.

The model does not have to be scientifically proven, but it does have to be built. In the following chapter we begin to lay the foundation.

1 Your Stance

No wind favors him who has no destined port.
—Michel de Montagne,
Sixteenth-century French essayist

See if this sounds familiar. You're waiting to interview someone and his secretary asks you, "What's your angle? How are you writing this?"

And you answer, "I don't know yet. I'm just trying to find out what's happening."

You're lying. To the secretary and—whether or not you realize it—to yourself.

Editors relentlessly insist that reporters walk into each new assignment with no preconceptions. What's ironic—and what most editors never mention—is that the best reporters purposely begin shaping biases as soon as they begin gathering facts on a particular assignment. This is part of their response to the staggering complexity of the world they have to cover. To succeed, they have developed a sophisticated information-processing system, one that takes fullest advantage of the human brain's natural ability to organize. The care they have used in building this system is what allows them to squeeze out every drop of their talent.

It's vital to understand how a skilled reporter focuses his powers of attention—how he listens and reads. His ability to string words together and organize facts on paper will be crippled if he does not psych himself into the correct attitude—the proper *stance*—for the gathering of information.

The skilled reporter is aware that his mind can successfully process only a certain amount of data. To compensate for that limitation he assumes a mental posture of arrogance. He virtually dares any source to provide him with usable information. On the outside, he may appear to have the patience of a saint, but inside his attitude toward extraneous information is harsh.

At the start of each coverage situation, to help himself look for the kind of information he needs, he begins building a running mental hypothesis—a crude outline, a sense of where the story is headed. Each piece of new information either helps confirm that hypothesis or persuades the reporter to modify his impression of the story as a whole.

This interplay between new data and a perceptual framework is a prime link in any skilled performance, from writing to bicycle riding. The most efficient performer has developed the fastest and most accurate system of what psychologists sometimes call perceptual coding.

The relationship between this natural ability and your own news-writing is clear: Be more conscious of sorting—"coding"—the information you collect as a reporter, and your ability to handle larger amounts of complex facts will improve.

Like many mental functions, perceptual coding is so obvious that its importance is often overlooked. Your brain groups and orders all data it confronts: Working through a still-mysterious filter that seems to protect its systems against overload, the brain takes new sensory information and links it to material stored in the memory. That puts the new data in perspective, setting the stage for action based on the new perception.

Your eyes are an example. What they see is merely an undefined collection of objects, but your visual system works with the brain to interpret the fragments and turn them into a coherent picture.

Almost subconsciously, the best reporters work the same way, always seeing the story in perspective. They build the frameworks of their stories—hypotheses—as soon as they begin working on them, comparing each new piece of information to the framework. In that way, they're able to keep their overall goal in sight, ask better questions, react more sharply to surprise answers, and constantly organize their information. Average reporters, on the other hand, often operate as little more than data collectors, and don't begin putting the information in perspective until they're driving back to the office or sitting down at the typewriter. By then it's often too late.

Remember, though, that he who lives by the framework can also die by it. To set up a story framework, you have to create a number of biases—temporary mental prejudices—against unrelated information. If you have made a mistake in your hypothesis, you will be perceiving your facts incorrectly, or looking for the wrong ones.

A skilled reporter avoids this pitfall by exploiting a parallel ability: acute sensitivity to any piece of information that contradicts his running hypothesis. He can set up a story framework early in the fact-gathering process because he is confident of his ability to adjust the framework in response to new evidence.

This process usually goes on with only the slightest external clues. A reporter who has mastered it may "feel" the story falling into place, but he rarely has the time to actively concentrate on whether each new piece of information confirms or modifies his hypothesis. He's too busy devoting most of his attention to asking a question or writing down an answer.

So don't be fooled by appearances. A reporter whose interview or research style looks disjointed may have organized his internal information-processing system superbly. That's what allows him to take more chances, ask more questions, grab at more straws during an interview, knowing all the while that his subconscious is meticulously sifting things. Ask him how he puts complicated stories in order and he may start talking about "good instincts."

Code word: "magic." My advice to you: Don't buy it.

You cannot throw a switch in your mind and suddenly possess the sophisticated attention mechanism of a skilled reporter. But you can, over a period of time, improve your mental process.

For example, examine how you use your powers of attention while you research or interview. How do you divide your attention between the piece of information you're looking at and the overall picture—the story framework?

This is the kind of thought strategy that most reporters never tackle. They're too overwhelmed or uninspired by the job to look inside themselves and consider what portions of their energy are reserved for various mental tasks and how they might improve. They consider a skill such as the power of attention to be much the same as the color of their eyes—a constant. It's not.

To control these kinds of variables, you begin slowly. You set a goal. For example, in interview situations the finest reporters are able to devote 90 percent of their attention to the question at hand, requiring only the remaining 10 percent to place that new information in perspective. Can you perform at that level automatically? Hell no. You have to put more effort into that latter chore—into figuring where your next question is coming from, into strengthening the links between incoming information from the interview subject and the storehouse of information in your memory.

To improve, concentrate at first on equally dividing your consciousness—50 percent to what you're hearing at the moment, 50 percent to asking yourself the supplementary question: How does this new information fit into the story? Gradually, you should need less of your mind to perform the perspective function.

Although newspaper reporting is not a profession—it's a craft, like making leather sandals—there are times when the level of required skill is as high as that of any of the so-called professions. This process of quickly comparing each fact to the big picture is one of them. Here the reporter works with the same sharp-edged intensity as the biochemist hunched over a microscope, instinctively weighing each fact against her running hypothesis. One piece of information tends to confirm it; another modifies it; yet another triggers the need for more evidence.

Think about this kind of skill the next time you observe a professional reporter in action. Watch her ask questions. Note her ability to interpret subtle shifts in the tone and direction of an interview or research, and to respond immediately either by modifying her hypothesis or leaning on the source.

Often, the source will want to change the subject prematurely. The skilled reporter senses that it's not time because her running hypothesis still seems valid and her need for evidence to confirm it remains unsatisfied.

For an example of what this process looks like when it works—and when it doesn't—we take you to police headquarters. We are watching the reporter, Ms. Mitchell, interview the local police chief, Captain Hendrix. In observing Mitchell, we will see that she has either an unsatisfactory grasp of where she wants the interview to go, or an insufficient amount of guts to raise a decent follow-up question:

MITCHELL: Let's talk about the police shootings. Officers killed sixteen suspects in the past year—twice as many as the year before—and the police commission last month approved a stricter policy on when an officer can fire his gun. How will officers adjust, and what's your feeling about the new policy?

HENDRIX: We're cops, and we know the commission is the head of the department. We know the rules. We'll follow them. We'll probably respond by holding a training seminar for all our officers.

MITCHELL: When will that be?

HENDRIX: In about a month. I feel it's important for each officer to know the changes that have come down, in terms of policy.

Wait a minute, Mitchell. Does the chief of police agree with the new shooting policy or doesn't he? In the back of Mitchell's mind, a red light or siren should have gone off as soon as Hendrix began talking about compliance with the policy. The reporter should have been operating with a story framework that featured a big slot labeled "Chief's Opinion." And when it became obvious the chief would rather not give his opinion, Mitchell's subconscious mind should have reminded her conscious mind that the void in the framework remained. She should have responded.

It should have happened like this:

HENDRIX: We're cops, and we know the commission is the head of the department. We know the rules. We'll follow them. We'll probably respond by holding a training seminar for all our officers.

MITCHELL: Let me ask you specifically: Do you like the new shooting policy?

HENDRIX: Well, I think it demands too much of an officer and sets a standard of conduct that I'm not too certain he can comply with.

MITCHELL: It's too harsh?

HENDRIX: Yes, it's too harsh.

MITCHELL: Why?

Let's hand the interview back to Mitchell at this point and see what she makes of it. Chief Hendrix answers the question about why the new shooting policy is too harsh:

HENDRIX: Police officers get paid to do a job. They are not robots. They are not perfect. If you look at our record of shootings over the past five years, you can see that.

MITCHELL: What were the numbers?

HENDRIX: Well, you mentioned there were sixteen in '99 and eight in '98. In 1997, there were . . .

Too bad. Our reporter lost track again because her mind didn't flash a warning signal when the chief offered only a vague, emotional reason for his dislike of the new policy. That slot in the story framework, "Chief's Opinion," needs fleshing out the way any other opinion does. A complete "why" is as important as "yes" or "no." When Mitchell heard the generalized answer to her question about why the new policy was too harsh, she should have felt the tug of her story's framework. The void had still not been completely taken care of. She should have trusted her memory to come back for the statistics of the past five years later in the interview. She should not have let the chief slip away. Something like this should have taken place:

HENDRIX: Yes, it's too harsh.

MITCHELL: Why?

HENDRIX: Police officers get paid to do a job. They are not robots. They are not perfect. If you look at our record of shootings over the past five years, you can see that.

MITCHELL: I want to make sure I understand what you're saying. Specifically, show me how an officer can't do his job just as well while conforming to the new policy.

HENDRIX: Well, take a fleeing felon. The new policy says we cannot shoot him. I believe if an officer has seen the felony suspect commit the act in question, and makes a persistent, audible demand for him to halt, and the suspect does not, then the officer should be allowed to fire with intent only to wound. Without that prerogative, I fear for the safety of those whom that fleeing felon may next attack. . . .

A better internal sense of where the story was going—the ability to see the story as a whole—would have allowed reporter Mitchell to ask questions that produced those two key answers: (1) The chief doesn't like the new policy, and (2) He's worried about an increase in crime as a result of it. Perhaps Mitchell would have run into those observations by accident later in the interview—but not if the chief didn't want her to. Clearly, the source, not the reporter, was in control of that interview.

Here is a personal consequence of failing to work from a story framework: The congressman who represented my old newspaper's district died unexpectedly. In putting together the story I made a few phone calls seeking comments from his close political associates. One call went to a local state senator. While we were chatting, I asked if he knew the time frame for the governor to call a special election to fill the remainder of the congressman's term. The senator knew the procedure in fine detail. I thanked him and turned to my other calls. A half hour later he called me back and said, "Say, you didn't ask me about this, but I thought you'd be interested: I'll probably run for that seat."

Now, how could I have forgotten to ask him whether he would run? By working on a story at a scattershot pace, by telling myself that I'd "put it all together" as soon as I'd made the last call, that's how. If I had been concentrating, I would have begun shaping a story framework in my mind as soon as I began making the calls, as illustrated by Diagram 1.1. A big fat space would have been set aside in the framework for the obvious question: Who'll replace him? The minute the state senator started rattling off the election procedure so precisely, that slot in the framework would have tugged on my attention. I would have been forced to ask myself, Why does this guy know so much about the dates? Why else?

We used the word *arrogance* earlier in describing the attitude a reporter must take in a news world glutted with information. Don't forget it. That's your stance: arrogance motivated by confidence. You know why you're covering this particular story, you know what information is likely to be significant, and you know you have only so much time and newspaper space.

In a business in which everybody wants your ear, you have to take the offensive. You have to play the news, or else it will play you. Outwardly, be as polite or naive or condescending or humble as your purposes demand, but inside your gut there has to be a nasty little man (about 5'2" with a goatee, too much nostril hair, and a British accent) eternally imploring each source, "Get to the *point*, man. Get *on* with it! Oh, *that's* not important. . . ."

STORY FRAMEWORK

When did he die?	Reactions from his associates	Capsule history of his accomplishments	Who'll replace him?	Process for selecting his replacement

DIAGRAM 1.1 In this story, a congressman has died unexpectedly. As the reporter begins gathering information, broad, primary issues in the story are first organized in this fashion, with each issue given a crude title and then cataloged, but not in any order of importance. This creates a rough guide to help the reporter search for relevant facts.

Your little man must personify that arrogance. He is the keeper of the door that leads to your mental shelves.

Shelves? The image is not important; the concept is. Your ability to construct a story framework has solved some problems. It has allowed you to mentally keep the entire story in front of you, rather than dealing with isolated facts, as you interview or do research. It has helped you decide what to look for, but it has not resolved the next consideration: How do you handle the information you find?

You don't simply begin writing the story. Subconsciously, each reporter uses some sort of mental trick—sometimes crude, sometimes refined—to mentally stack the incoming facts in the order he plans to use them. He must begin doing this as soon as he encounters any new information. If he waits until he begins to write, he's dead.

The construction of a story framework can be envisioned as the placement of the anticipated prime facts in a horizontal line. No priorities are set; the reporter is merely making a mental list of the facts he thinks he will have to gather.

But once he begins collecting those prime facts, decisions have to be made. He arranges the material in what can be thought of as a rough vertical pattern: good stuff on top, bad stuff on the bottom.

There is no prescribed method for this sort of mind game, but at the same time there is no way a reporter can put together a complicated story without going through such a prewriting process, consciously or otherwise. The earlier he begins stacking his facts in his mind, the better off he will be.

The variables in this process are endless, and you should examine your own. Can you assign different facts to different levels or categories in your mind? Do you feel able to shift facts from one level to another if new developments occur? Do you find your own process working more keenly when you are suddenly snowed under with information—say, at a city council hearing when a batch of government reports and public speakers all converge on the same issue? Sure, you take notes, but your head is what usually holds the broad outline of the story. How well do you organize the information that flows in?

One method, modeled loosely on a technique I found myself using subconsciously after a number of years as a reporter is shown in Diagram 1.2.

There is an initial "yes/no" filter somewhere in my mind, or so I pretend. It screens each piece of new information to see whether it fits into the story that is developing. "Yes" material—facts, quotes, or other data that seem to have a chance of helping the story—goes to one of several shelves in a "yes" column. The top "yes" shelf is the most important one; I have tried to wipe it clean so that prime facts for only this story will be placed there.

The other "yes" shelves hold lower-priority information, in descending order of importance. Standing parallel to the "yes" shelves are the "no" shelves; most "no" information—data judged to be irrelevant to the story—is stacked here. I do not pay attention to it, although I know that most of it will make its way into my long-term memory, and that some of it will pop back into my consciousness in the future.

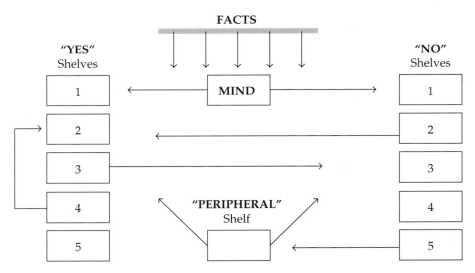

DIAGRAM 1.2   As individual facts are collected, the reporter makes a quick, initial determination of the relevance of each one. Is the information usable or not? Roughly, what is its priority? Subsequent facts may force changes in the position of facts that have been stacked in one of three sets of mental shelves—"Yes," "No," and "Peripheral."

Some information I receive doesn't scream out for a particular shelf in my mind, so it is assigned to a shelf standing between the "yes" and "no" columns, a "peripheral" shelf. New circumstances may require information from this shelf to be retrieved and compared with facts on the "yes" or "no" shelves, and possibly to be moved onto one of those shelves.

Your mental filing system must be flexible. It does not have to be used with equal intensity in all coverage situations. But it must be ready. Only a reporter with a well-organized mind can master a story in which a fascinating twist of events or unusual human drama is shrouded by complex circumstances. The average reporter is not mentally equipped for such an expedition.

How literally should you try to use a filing system? To the extent that it helps you. How much can you influence it? Plenty. Take the peripheral shelf. What's important here is to exploit background or semi-related information to the fullest degree. When you get an assignment, it is mandatory that you put your peripheral shelf in good order by checking your memory and your paper's library to see if there is relevant background information available. This can be done before you begin building your story framework, and from there a chain reaction takes place: A better framework helps you ask better questions; better questions produce better information to file on your mental shelves.

Like most good ideas, mental organization is an old one. Seventeenth-century scientist-philosopher René Descartes likened the mind to a room, and pointed out that it could be neat or untidy. Obviously, you can find things much more easily in a well-ordered room.

If you're patient enough to push through the wordy translation of Descartes's "Rules for the Direction of the Mind," you can develop a feeling for the kind of mental organization he advocated:

> If I have first found out by separate mental operations what the relation is between the magnitudes A and B, then between B and C, between C and D, and finally between D and E—that does not entail my seeing what the relation is between A and E. Nor can the truths previously learned give me a precise knowledge of it unless I recall them all.
>
> To remedy this, I would run them over from time to time, keeping the imagination moving continuously in such a way that while it is intuitively perceiving each fact, it simultaneously passes on to the next. This I would do until I had learned to pass from the first to the last so quickly that no stage in the process was left to the care of the memory. [Instead] I seemed to have the whole in intuition before me at the same time. This method will relieve memory, diminish the sluggishness of our thinking, and definitely enlarge our mental capacity.

Psych yourself into the necessary state of concentration. Conceive of your attention as a beam of light, which can be focused as sharply as needed on incoming information; or envision your mind as a computer, neatly processing each new fact through rigid news standards, then flipping each fact like a card into a precise mental slot, to be retrieved when circumstances dictate; or picture your progress by telling yourself that improved mental organization is allowing the neurons in your brain to fire correct decisions more quickly than before.

Have an image, and remember: It doesn't do any good to have your laptop charged up and ready to go unless you have kept your shelves tidy.

Now, step inside the newsroom, where we'll watch an artist at work on one of the most basic mental filters—the "lead" filter.

More on "Your Stance" in the Appendix:

- Four reporters give you tips on how to come up with good story ideas
- A sermon on the gospel of detail
- The art of showing versus telling

CHAPTER

2 Leads

Meet Ms. Turner. She is a fictitious character who will appear in our newsroom from time to time to illustrate how newsthinking strategies are put to work. Her attributes symbolize the level of performance we want to shoot for.

Ms. Turner is, among other things, a merchant of leads—the crisp opening paragraphs of a breaking story, the unexpected, twisting, graph-to-graph dance that opens a feature, the heartbreaking ache that introduces the sob story. She's the one everybody in the office seems to seek out at one time or another with a story they can't solve, a story that seems to defy a clever or sensitive lead—and she always seems to deliver. As a result, she's regarded as sort of a doctor of words, but she's really more of a mechanic. Her genius in constructing lead paragraphs lies in her ability to grasp the structure of a story—to take it apart and put it back together, to distill how the parts form the whole. She compares the elements that make the story newsworthy, analyzes their importance, mentally extracts the essence of the story, and then translates that impression into words.

Our description of how she does it is going to sound complex, but like any skilled performer, Ms. Turner has taught her brain to make clusters of mental movements rather than one decision at a time. Sometimes a lead may come to her in ten seconds; other times it may take ten minutes, or perhaps two hours, of frustrated thinking. Regardless, she subconsciously runs each lead through the same mental process, and then compares her results with her original concept of what the lead paragraphs should accomplish.

In doing that, she is utilizing our system of mental filters—checkpoints along the route that each story travels through her mind. In Chapter 1, we saw how a skilled reporter sets up a "stance" filter to evaluate and organize incoming information. In this chapter, we will construct the first of many mental filters that come into play when you compose your story.

The "lead" filter will force every lead to pass a series of tough tests—and it will force you to begin rewriting if the lead doesn't pass them.

(Remember, the order in which a reporter's mind operates is always subject to change. In some instances, he establishes the sequence of the entire story and then concentrates on the lead. In other cases, the process is reversed. We'll work under the latter assumption, and will study sequencing of the overall story in Chapter 3.)

No matter what kind of story Ms. Turner is trying to write, her goals in shaping the lead are constant. The broadest one: She wants to feel herself closing the gap between the essence of what she knows (her thoughts) and the lead that will appear on paper (her words). She envisions the creation of an image (the lead) that will slide precisely over the essence—writing matched perfectly to reality. She doesn't kid herself. She knows this is not always possible.

Before she begins composing, she analyzes the story elements she collected earlier. Her memory runs over the prime facts. It also reviews the story framework she employed during the information-gathering process. The framework kept her conscious of where the story was heading; now her analysis prompts her to ask, "Where has the story wound up? How has it evolved?"

Her ability to see parts and wholes has taught her that nearly all stories share certain characteristics. For example:

- Conflict: people against each other; people against a system; a person in conflict with his beliefs, having to make a difficult decision; people in conflict with events beyond their control.
- Impact on readers: it can be direct (property assessments are up 30 percent) or indirect (the high crime rate is cutting tourism).
- Purely interesting information: silly, warm, dramatic, pathetic, unique. The intensity of these nonconflict, nonimpact elements is a key to any good feature story.

Ms. Turner examines her prime facts to find where each of these and other characteristics surfaces. She tries to develop a sense of how much of a role each characteristic plays in this story. Which surfaces most frequently? Which offers the most power? Which characteristic best represents the essence of the story? Which best ties in with her goals for this story?

She never anticipates black-and-white answers to these questions. She often expects to find merely an impulse, rather than a strategy she could put into words. She is simply taking advantage of her finely tuned mind—in effect, hitting a mental trigger that launches a myriad of alternatives. Sometimes the facts are easy to handle and her choice of leads is obvious and instantaneous. Other times, she plays the alternatives against each other, waiting for an angle to pop out, as though the collision between the merging facts and her own news values will somehow force the correct choice into the open.

Finally, the angle comes. She knows the direction her lead will take. Now she composes it word by word, in her head or on the screen, and the process of feedback begins. She compares the lead with those original goals: Why is the story being written, and for whom? How successfully does the lead represent the essence of the story? If the lead is indirect (for example, an anecdotal lead), how well does it draw the reader into the essence?

Now comes a complex, internal juggling act that has been built and refined thousands of times by years of trial and error. Turner cannot describe this stage very well, but inside she knows when it's clicking. It allows her to rapidly weigh the value of each element in her lead; to ponder which ones may have to be sacrificed or changed; to shuffle the elements to form new combinations; and, finally, to make her choices. Maybe the first lead she thought of was the right one. Maybe another version works better. Maybe none of them do, forcing her to start over. If the feedback she gets from putting the lead through her filter is positive, she continues to compose the remainder of the story. If she receives negative feedback, she goes back to square one.

Does the word *feedback* bother you? Are you weary of jargon from the social sciences and engineering creeping into your artistry? Well, hang on. The concept is vital to your ability to improve. It is only through the constant, unspoken use of feedback that reporters like Ms. Turner seem to effortlessly crank out superb leads. They have constructed a mental loop that forces every key thought to be tested—to be fed back for analysis—before it is put on paper.

Next time you hear a reporter whining for the tenth time in an hour and a half about his "writer's block," remember what's probably happening inside him. It's not that the words won't come; his mind is producing plenty of combinations of words. The problem is that each new combination of words that his mind produces is being tested against his lead filter—and is promptly dashed against the rocks. It's not that nothing's coming, it's that nothing works.

And so it is with Ms. Turner. Do you know the feeling of simply typing out whatever comes to mind? Of letting the wave of words spill out and crash against the screen? Turner doesn't. She is one of the most calculating people you have ever met. Before any thought is turned into a typing impulse, it is double-checked. Diagram 2.1 illustrates the process. The style of simply letting the words flow out, on the other hand, would look like Diagram 2.2. See? In the latter example, there is no quality control.

If the reporter who just "lets it flow" were a machine, he'd be an electric fan, blowing his energy into space. If you played the same analogy game with Ms. Turner, she'd be an air conditioning system, constantly monitoring the temperature, feeding back the information to a central control mechanism, which then adjusts the room temperature to the system's goal—say, 70 degrees.

Take a second and pick up something, such as a magazine. As you move, your brain is sending motor impulses to contract the proper muscles.

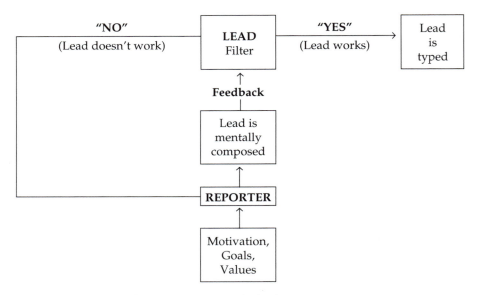

DIAGRAM 2.1   How feedback improves the lead.

DIAGRAM 2.2   A weaker process—there's no feedback.

As your muscles contract, sense organs send feedback impulses (via the sensory fibers) to your central nervous system, informing it of the degree of muscle action. Your brain responds by modulating or inhibiting further motor impulses until your hand closes around the magazine and lifts it. You take such a gesture for granted because you rarely fail at it, but in fact your system made constant checks each tiny step of the way. It measured each step against the goal of picking up the magazine; it closed the gap between the current state and the desired performance.

As we've seen, Ms. Turner's writing process works the same way. It works because she is conscious of the need to make choices. Yet it is not merely the choices that make Turner's work great, but the way she makes them. And it is here that most of us, in our formal education as reporters and writers, have been led astray. We have been trained to be average. We have been trained to think that we can match certain types of writing with certain circumstances. We have been given the impression that we can work through formulas. We have been told to sit down with books containing great newspaper lead paragraphs and analyze the styles, and then we have been lectured about the kinds of circumstances we'll probably face on the job, and how we'll mesh style with situation.

Presto! The creation of a crude thought process. Most of the time in the news business it will work; the reporter will make the right choice. But what happens when events start occurring in ways that defy the probabilities he has memorized? What does he fall back on?

His butt, that's what. He's in no position to judge the story on its own merits because he has been conditioned to see "types" of stories, and react: an anecdotal lead for one set of circumstances, a quote lead for another, an extremely terse lead for a third, a question-and-answer-type lead for a fourth.

Very, very crude. And that's what's behind so many editors' frustrations with reporters who can't seem to hit the mark when they tackle a difficult story.

Listen: Nobody can teach you how to write by simply showing you how words interact. It doesn't mean anything unless you can grab the reporter who wrote the words and ask, "Why? How did you make your choices?" You have to understand how his *thoughts* interacted to produce those words. You have to look at the causes, not merely the effects.

You can skim over a thousand examples of good leads and bad ones, and you can know the components of each, but that doesn't build your ability to make tough choices. It doesn't prepare you for the future. If anything, it produces a false sense of assurance that circumstances will fall into place, and that a certain type of lead will work. Sorry. Those styles of leads that look good now will develop weak spots when you apply them to tomorrow's news—new events, new components, new choices.

You cannot control the news, so you must compensate by developing sophisticated techniques to control the way you process it. Turner's ability to understand structure is the main plank, but there are two other peripheral considerations that go into each lead.

The first is a sense of values. You must instinctively pose a series of questions before you start composing: What is the purpose of this story? Who is it aimed at? What am I trying to accomplish? Hardest of all, you have to mean it.

Good writers don't have to consciously ask these questions; they flash on as part of the normal work orientation, the way the feeling of settling yourself in your chair tells you you're ready to begin typing. There are tough side questions, too: Do I need to make one last phone call? (After all, it's nearly 10 P.M.) Do I need to check the library again? (I've already checked it three times on this story.) Should I go to that meeting? (It's important, but it's on a Sunday.)

If you aren't asking yourself those kinds of questions before you start composing, start asking them. If you haven't built up the values that make those kinds of questions important, start planning another career.

The final consideration in writing the right kind of leads is a sense of exploitation. The word has an unpleasant connotation, but let it be. The hard truth is that in order to compensate for all the pressures against good writing in the news business, you have to push the facts as far as you can without violating the essence of the story or your own ethics. You have to develop the ability to squeeze out the juiciest, most interesting material. You have to be ready to pounce.

You may not want to admit this to many people outside the news business, but it's a fact of life. Look what your writing is up against—the pressure of deadline; the pressure of mediocre editors who don't understand the craft of writing and fall back on clever phrases such as "Just tell the story"; the pressure to play it safe.

These institutionalized pressures push down on you; they conspire to flatten your writing, to produce the sameness that marks most news stories. You have to push up—fight against the pressure, overcompensate. Usually, you'll have to do so on your own, because once an editor on deadline judges a story to be accurate and functional, he'll usually buy it and begin editing it for grammar and interior phrasing. He rarely possesses the time or patience to consider restructuring it.

Let's put you on the job for an example. It's Tuesday and you work for a daily newspaper in Los Angeles. On Monday, a plane crashed after a flawed takeoff. On Tuesday, the survivors become available, and you score the best interview, winning you the right to write a sidebar. You hand it in. The city editor begins skimming it:

> The chilling events of Monday's Continental Airlines Boeing 767 crash at Los Angeles International Airport are still starkly vivid in the mind of John Simmons.

Simmons, 58, was aboard the 9:23 flight bound for Honolulu, Hawaii. He sat in his living room Tuesday and recounted in a calm, steady voice the details of the crash that killed two persons and injured 74 others, but left him unharmed.

"I had an aisle seat on the right-hand side of the plane, near the front," he said. "I remember an escape hatch 12 or 15 feet in front of me.

"I felt the first tire blow. It felt just like a blowout on a car. Then, I guess the pilot applied his brakes. You know, that puts a tremendous amount of pressure on the other tires. I'm sure I heard at least three more tires blow. But I never anticipated there would be so much damage."

At this point the city editor ought to look up, open his mouth and bite your head off. How in the world could you fail to exploit a quote as juicy as "It felt just like a blowout on a car"? What a striking conflict between a man's impressions and reality. It's a description that puts your readers in the shoes of the passengers. You can sacrifice the date, make of airplane and location from your first paragraph; anybody who read today's paper already knows that. Your strategy on this story is almost mathematical: Your ability to play with the structure of a lead is directly proportional to your audience's familiarity with the circumstances. So play!

You would never have written a lead that average if you had set specific goals for the story, based on what your audience knew and what you wanted to achieve—a sidebar about what the passengers experienced—and if you had been conscious of the need to exploit your best material.

Ideally, your city editor understands these principles. And after he chews you out, he takes the time to type out the lead combination that screamed to be written:

"It felt just like a blowout on a car," John Simmons said.

It wound up being far more explosive.

Simmons, 58, a survivor in Monday's Continental Airlines Boeing 767 crash at Los Angeles International Airport, remained stunned Tuesday by the toll of the incident.

"I felt the first tire blow," he said. Then came what he assumed was the jolt of the plane's brakes. "You know, that puts a tremendous amount of pressure on. . . ."

But you can rarely depend on your editors to improve a story like that; you have to take the responsibility. Your success in print depends on how well you use your filters.

Now that you are conscious of developing a filter for your leads, we turn to a broader problem: developing the overall sequence of the story. As we noted earlier in this chapter, leads and sequencing are intertwined. Both processes involve the ability to shuffle and sacrifice elements, to set a goal and focus on it. Neither process can be easily taught, because each is based on a reporter's willingness to push himself, to tell himself flatly, "That's not good enough"—even when he wishes desperately that it were.

More on "The Lead" in the Appendix:

- Bringing a sense of urgency to anecdotal leads
- Keeping dependent clauses in check

3 Sequencing

Within the unconscious, an automatic combining and recombining takes place until certain combinations having a peculiar affinity for our emotional consciousness occur, and bring themselves to our attention.

—Jules-Henri Poincaré,
Nineteenth century French mathematician

Everything is connected.

—A subject in a contemporary experiment in biophysics, describing her feelings during a "felt shift," a period of mental insight believed to represent higher-level reorganization in the brain.

All newswriters, no matter what their deficiencies, can empathize with the words of both the "felt shift" subject and Poincaré. Everyone, at least occasionally, has had that feeling of his story suddenly falling together, each paragraph tumbling into place. Like the other skills we've discussed, it isn't magic; the best reporters take certain steps to achieve this organization.

Let's pick up where we left off in Chapter 2. The lead has been transferred from your head to the screen. Now what? You're pausing, and the pause begins to grow uncomfortably long. Unconsciously, you may be hoping to become caught up in a process described by the late B. F. Skinner, a controversial American experimental psychologist who explained all human behavior in terms of stimulus, response, and reward for success. "As we write a paragraph," Skinner said, "we create an elaborate chain of verbal stimuli which alter the probabilities of other words to follow."

All newswriters have experienced this phenomenon. We count on the lead to spark mysterious rhythms that will propel the rest of the story, bringing forth the paragraphs in the right order.

And like all long-shot bets, it sometimes works. Writing the story one thought after another, seemingly without overview or preparation, is not impossible. But remember: When the technique doesn't work, you tend to look like an idiot in the eyes of your editor and readers.

A good reporter often fools her colleagues and herself by saying that she's banging out a story without formally organizing it, when in fact she has subconsciously put the story through a sophisticated set of organizational filters.

That's what we're looking at in this chapter: the most crucial component of solid news or feature writing—sequencing. The best reporters master it by increasing their ability to hold a complete story outline in their immediate memory. They operate on two levels simultaneously, writing each paragraph with regard to its interior structure and its role in the story as a whole. They utilize written outlines, certainly, but the initial work—the mental spadework—is what produces the brilliance.

It is achieved by continuing the process we discussed earlier. The prime facts in the story have already been crudely sorted while the reporter gathered information, and they were roughly reviewed again when she wrote the lead. Now the process of putting the information in order must become more delicate. The facts must be viewed for their relationship to one another. The chronology must sometimes be discarded and replaced by an outline of facts that emphasizes the essence of the story rather than merely the order in which events happened.

With that mental outline prepared, the reporter begins typing, pausing for countless brief interludes in which she scans that outline to make sure the paragraphs are being ordered correctly. So highly tuned is this skill that some reporters insist they bring up each paragraph from a deep, dark well that they do not understand. These are the people who cruise through a sparkling 800-word story in the last forty-five minutes of deadline and confound you that night by saying, "Man, it was flowing good today."

Obviously, the inborn quality of that reporter's mind has something to do with her ability to hold a great deal of organized data in mental limbo for instant recall. But God-given ability is only part of the story; the newspaper world is filled with reporters who don't pay regard to the development of this skill, who don't try to incorporate it, who too often work from paragraph to paragraph, waiting for that infrequent sensation of the story falling together. It doesn't come unless you concentrate, and the reporters who don't concentrate on improving their sequencing abilities are often the ones who receive the most elementary assignments: Their editors grow convinced that they simply don't have the brains to handle complex stories.

To improve, you must first consider the mental attitudes that produce good sequencing, and then apply them throughout each coverage situation —not merely when you sit down at the computer.

Sequencing is a mental act that follows a natural process in the brain which psychologists call integration—recognizing that various parts would form a unified pattern if they were all shown together. For example, when you look at a truck, you don't see all the relevant details at a single glance. Your eyes rove over it, observing first one part, then another. Your total perception is not the same as the result of any one glance, but rather a product built by integrating the data from many different glances. If your visual system is working properly, you see that the trailer is linked by a heavy metal brace to the cab; if there's something wrong with your system, perhaps you see two separate vehicles. Similarly, if your sequencing system is working, you will be able to combine two seemingly disparate comments that were made a half hour apart in a press conference; your sense of overview will find that they belong together. If your sequencing skills aren't developed highly enough, you'll miss the connection.

Sequencing is not merely a two-gear process, in which overview and immediacy must mesh. There are a number of mental attitudes—a number of mini-filters—operating at once. They put simultaneous pressure on you to organize your story with respect to various newswriting values. The skilled reporter stands out because he has learned to balance these attitudes instinctively, so that each provides the proper tug on his attention while he writes. Average reporters may be conscious of these tugs, but they respond more crudely, sometimes overcompensating and thus throwing their writing out of kilter. The reason there is no limit to the mastery of newsthinking is that there is no limit to the precision with which these sequencing attitudes can interact.

It's important to understand that no two reporters would use the same terms to define this balancing act. We all have trouble describing such delicate professional mechanisms. And we each tend to emphasize different natural processes in evaluating how well our writing systems are working at a given moment.

Some reporters—myself included—are most conscious of their kinetic systems (body motion) when they write. They measure their effectiveness by the way it "feels"—the rhythm, the subtle physical movements. It's a rather fuzzy standard, but the writer learns to trust it. As an example, I remember periods of remarkable speed, clarity, and verbal unity at the keyboard during which I began feeling like Ray Charles at the piano—strong, distinctive rhythm, inexorable flow of words. For a while, that feeling became a standard, a level to compare myself with. But not all writers check their writing process that way. Some emphasize their auditory systems, measuring their performance by the way the story sounds in their inner voice (see Chapter 6) or how the clicking of the keys sounds to their ear; others are most conscious of visualizing the words in their heads and judge their effectiveness by the clarity with which that process takes place.

Listen as the late novelist James Michener illustrates the diversity:

If I had a daughter or son determined to be a writer . . . naturally I'd expect them to be competent in their own language and to know something about psychology and the history of what fine writers have accomplished in the past. But the two courses I'd make obligatory would be one in ceramics, so that you could feel form emerging from inchoate clay. I think this is very important, that you have a feeling for form and a sense of how it's achieved.

And the second course would be eurhythmic dancing, so that you could feel within your own body the capacity that you have for movement and form and dramatic shifts in perspective. Of course, if you can't locate a class in such dancing, you might pick up the same sensations in a long game of basketball or tennis, where the ebb and flow of movement is pronounced. Or perhaps in any other sport requiring bold shifts of movement.

What the artist requires is a sense of emerging form, a kinesthetic sense of what the human body is capable of. If you marry those sensory capabilities to a first-rate brain, you have a good chance of becoming an artist.

Within any system that a reporter uses to tell himself whether a story is flowing properly, there may be hundreds of individualized tricks or tip-offs. These differences are a major reason why it's pointless for anyone to offer the ultimate description of how good writing should "feel."

Nevertheless, one step is always there: the process of feeding back the chosen order of paragraphs through a sequencing filter. Every few paragraphs, the big question must be answered: Is the sequence working? The mechanism is similar to, though more complex than, the filter for leads that was analyzed in Chapter 2.

First, you choose the prime facts you feel are needed for the story; then you give each prime fact a code word—one short word that symbolizes the information—to make mental and handwritten outlining more streamlined; then you pick an order for the prime facts, trying to determine how many paragraphs will be required to develop each fact.

Now you begin typing, developing each fact—but before you get too far, stop. Feed your copy back through your mind's sequencing filter. Does the story represent the essence of what you know? Is it going in the right direction? If the answer is yes, keep typing. If it's no, start over—and don't just start rewriting, start *rethinking*. Put yourself through the entire sequencing process again, as illustrated in Diagram 3.1.

There is no systematic guide to constructing a process like this, but try to build your own feedback style—with your own rules and tests—until you eventually begin shaping sharp outlines subconsciously. To get there, use these kinds of mental attitudes:

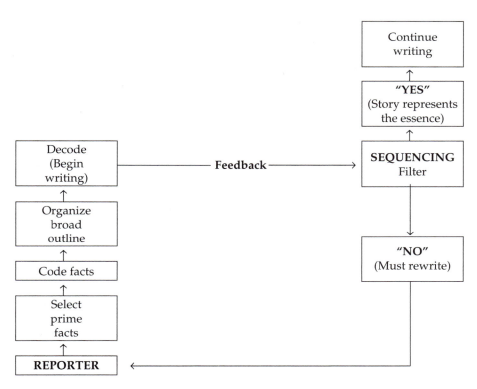

DIAGRAM 3.1   The sequencing process. If the reporter does not combine the paragraphs properly, his filter instructs him to try a new sequence.

Look for the pattern. If you built a proper framework to search for your facts and then diligently stored the facts in your mind, you're on your way. Still, you have to scan your primary and secondary facts again for relationships between them—connections that may have seemed unimportant when you were gathering the information.

Don't be a slave to chronology. Human nature and the pressures of news work conspire to tilt reporters toward writing stories based on the order in which they witnessed events. Many times, that's the only way a particular kind of story can be written.

The more crucial times are those when an average story—structured on the chronology the reporter witnessed—can be made better by decisively abandoning that order. You see examples of this restructuring all the time, but the effort it requires is often invisible; the better it's done, the easier it seems.

Example: You interview a county assessor who's under fire for unequal appraisal of property; then you interview three homeowners who want to recall him. Your story order runs something like this: a graph or two for the homeowners' general charges, then a graph or two for the assessor's response, then a list of specific charges, then a list of the assessor's specific responses.

That's average. Improving it is easy: Integrate the charges and responses so that each charge is immediately followed by the assessor's answer.

That's better, but the reporter who is willing to abandon the chronology can go even further—and in a completely fair manner. Remember the first sequencing attitude we mentioned: "Look for the pattern." If there are a dozen charges, see if they can be combined into four or five broader groups. Don't be satisfied with one alteration of the chronology; further modification is often essential in getting to the meat of a story.

Translate the essence.   Your ability to see patterns should have produced the insights that formed the roots of your story outline. From there, begin asking yourself some sharp questions. Precisely what is the *effect* of the merging of my facts? What does my story really say? Does my outline successfully translate what I *know* into the story? Does it communicate the *essence,* rather than just a handful of details?

When seeking the essence, the writer is prodded to go further than merely setting down one side of a story and then the other. He pushes himself to add perspective and depth to the structure of the report.

Develop the feeling of being ready to erupt volcanically. Try to gear yourself to react strongly when your mind reaches insights that strengthen the story outline. Have confidence that there is one best method of sequencing each story, and that you will recognize it when it suddenly appears from under the surface of your consciousness.

Isolate. To find that best outline, you have to narrow your focus. Decide which parts of the story are hardest to tell, and separate them from the remainder. The better you can isolate a problem, the more strongly your beam of concentration can tackle it. Ask yourself, What are the large problems in organizing this story? What are the small ones? What should I sacrifice? All problems have "fuzz" around them, which makes them appear large. Get rid of the fuzz and you'll become more aware of the core of the problem.

Scan your prime facts methodically before you begin to develop an outline. Break them down several ways. First, consider each prime fact; then create two piles of prime facts, the most usable in one, the rest in the other. Then sift through the most usable facts again, further limiting the number that are essential to the story. Again, develop your own organized process.

Eliminate broad classes of data and then narrower ones, until the final set of facts—the set of facts you will use—has been separated from everything else.

Think of yourself as a painter who instinctively strives for that fine line of balance between foreground drama and background detail. Unless you are conscious of attaining an artistic balance, you will fall into traps: lead paragraphs overloaded with detail; four-paragraph quotes that should have been cut down to two paragraphs; technical descriptions too high in the story, blocking the reader from continuing to follow the essence of your report.

Develop a rhythm in your phrasing. Try to blend long and short sentences and a variety of styles into this sequencing maneuver. Your mind should not be devoted solely to the ordering of facts when you build the outline; any offbeat phrasing techniques you may use will influence how well the sequence works.

Learn to say "no" to yourself. Develop the discipline to separate your good impulses from your bad ones. Many good ideas simply don't work well in a news framework or take exceptional talent to manipulate. Depend on your news values to warn you when a certain style of sequencing threatens to make the story misleading. You must be able to visualize the story as a whole, take a couple of steps back, and ponder its overall impact.

The difficulty in making these sequencing attitudes work together may be compared to bowling. Imagine yourself on a lane in a bowling alley. As you make your approach and throw the ball, you are making several calculations at once—eyes, arms, legs, head, each trying to combine with the actions of the others. People who bowl for fun have trouble improving their scores beyond a point because every time they adjust one part of their approach (such as the arm swing), it throws all the other components off. Professional bowlers are patient enough to tinker with each part of their game, making countless adjustments until each component is operating at ultimate effectiveness. Then they tinker some more to perfect the way each step blends with the others.

The mental attitudes that control sequencing must be properly coordinated in order to propel the facts (the bowling ball) down the lane to hit the reader (the pins) with maximum accuracy and impact.

Monitor your improvement in orchestrating the interplay among these attitudes. Be conscious of reaching a plateau, then leveling off, then climbing to a new, higher plateau, and so on. In working your way up to a new plateau, you will be slowly achieving the maximum development of one order of writing habits. Reaching the plateau means that that order has become sufficiently automatic for you to concentrate on a higher order of habits—the next plateau.

For example, consider a single sequencing attitude: the balancing of foreground and background information. For a month or two, a reporter who has not paid formal attention to this balance will have to prod himself to consider the relationship every time he writes a story. After a time, the balance factor will come to his mind automatically, and the calculation will be made seemingly by instinct. Now the reporter can use his energy to examine more sophisticated balance factors—for example, the relationship between information in the first two paragraphs—rather than the more crude balance between the two halves of the story.

Most skills in newsthinking seem to fall into this hierarchy of habits. When a reporter manages to sufficiently master a higher order of skill, the steps are "lost"—they remain, but they no longer must be taken consciously. They have been blended into her lower orders of habits, and serve as a foundation for progress to the next higher order. In the art of sequencing, that relationship explains why skilled reporters can produce a story without seeming to think about it. They have perfected even the highest-level writing habits, freeing themselves to focus most of their concentration on a relatively small number of sophisticated variables. A roster of difficult considerations is resolved immediately: the story is outlined in depth, shaped by attention to dozens of "outside" factors, such as the amount of space available, the deadline, the sensitivity of the assignment editor, the other stories the paper has published on this subject in the last two weeks and the amount of attention competing papers have paid to this story.

That's why a skilled reporter can be typing furiously with twenty-five pieces of notepaper strewn across his desk and a telephone clamped to his ear when he suddenly pauses, tells the caller to wait a minute, and shouts a question across the city room: "Is Smith's story coming in today, or is it holding?"

Background: The reporter knows his story and reporter Smith's are the last two to be turned in before deadline. His caller has provided a piece of information that can be developed to quickly supplement today's story—but not without using another eight or nine paragraphs. Is Smith's story going in today? If so, there's probably not enough space to warrant the extra time our reporter needs; he'll be better off using the time he has to polish up the story as it's now written. He can go after the new item separately for tomorrow's paper. But if Smith got tied up, the situation changes; our reporter will tell an editor about the potential addition and see if the desk wants it for today's edition.

What is sophisticated here is not the judgment itself, but the ability to make it amid deadline chaos. The habit of checking such factors in similar situations has been learned well enough to be triggered without conscious attention. That may not be a habit vital to pure writing, but its usefulness to newswriting is obvious.

Try, then, to reach plateaus in which you increase your ability to hold a broad outline in your head while playing those various sequencing attitudes against each other. Envision the small units that comprise your basic skills. Try to feel as though you are combining those units, so that they begin to happen in bursts of threes and fours—or tens and twenties—leaving you free to concentrate on bigger questions. Among the biggest: that quick, back-and-forth shift between the paragraph or sentence just coming onto the paper and The Big Picture—your mental overview that dictates how your paragraphs should be combined.

Now it's time to venture into more murky but equally vital territory: knowing your reader.

More on "Sequencing" in the Appendix:

- Using your oral skills to prepare for the writing stage
- Altering your sentence rhythm
- Stories that prosper through the power of ideas, not mere quotes or wordplay

CHAPTER

4 Knowing the Reader

A few days from now, when you're in the midst of typing, stop long enough to challenge yourself with this question: Why would anyone want to read that story you're writing?

Before you answer, consider the waggle dance of the honeybee. First decoded in 1945, the dance is one of the most complex of all animal communications systems. It goes like this:

When a foraging worker bee returns from the field after discovering a food source or desirable new nest site at some distance from the hive, it indicates the location of this target to its fellow workers by performing.

The pattern of the bee's movement is a figure 8, repeated over and over again amid crowds of other workers. The most distinctive and informative element of the dance is the "straight run" (the middle of the figure 8), which is given emphasis by the waggle, a rapid vibration of the body. The complete shake of the body is performed thirteen to fifteen times per second, and at the same time the bee emits an audible buzzing sound by vibrating its wings. The straight run represents a miniaturized version of the flight from the hive to the target. It points directly at the target if the bee is dancing outside the hive on a horizontal surface. If the bee is on a vertical surface inside the hive, the straight run points at the appropriate angle away from the vertical surface. Gravity and the position of the sun are used as orientation cues. The straight run also provides information on the distance of the target from the hive, which is often accurate to within 20 percent, scientists say.

Now, the bee's techniques may seem to rival the more advanced properties of our language, but in fact they don't come close. We simply take too many of the complexities and pitfalls of the English language for granted, and therein lies the rationale for the next two mental filters we need to build: one that forces you to work with a sense of your audience, and another that forces you to inject perspective into your work. The latter will be covered in Chapter 5.

When you compare the waggle dance of the honeybee to the waggle dance of the human brain and tongue, the bee's version becomes a pretty simple affair. The straight run of the bee is, after all, merely an enactment of the flight the bees will take. The rules are always fixed, and the messages are always literal: they cannot be manipulated to provide new forms of information.

Your newswriting, on the other hand, is based on rules of linguistics which only the most advanced specialists care to fathom. Those rules—and those of our culture—provide us with a vastly larger array of messages than is provided by the mere presumed meanings of the words themselves. In addition, you can project an endless number of nonliteral images—fiction, lies, demagoguery—by the way you inform the listener or reader of your intent.

The possibilities are endless. Endless enough, certainly, to explain why so many newswriters get into trouble and can't provide their readers with a clear image. But by knowing your audience, you make the first move toward limiting the variables, toward isolating the target, toward narrowing the odds of miscommunicating. To the degree you are able to visualize your reader, you're developing another valuable test of what information to cut from your story, what to keep and how to sequence it.

You cannot succeed as a newswriter without developing this "readership" filter, this chore of perpetually asking yourself, Who's reading this, and what does he know? To ignore it is to proceed with an inflated idea of how a subscriber perceives your publication.

Don't kid yourself. No matter how important your newspaper or magazine or book is to you, it is no more than one of dozens of items on the periphery of the reader's consciousness. He rarely has the patience that many reporters' writing seems to demand.

It is not merely great writers who take pains to construct this filter; all great artists are aware of it. Listen to the late composer Richard Rodgers:

> All I really want to do is to provide a hardworking man in the blouse business with a method of expressing himself. If he likes a tune, he can whistle it, and it will make his life happier. . . .

Or actor and director Gene Wilder:

> I make movies for a fat lady in Kansas City. I imagine her weighing 280 pounds; I can picture her swatting flies on a hot summer's day and going to the movies every Friday night. And coming away saying, "Boy, did I have a good time. Did I laugh! Did I cry!"

Odd things happen to news stories when the readership filter isn't used. For example:

■ A story reports a price feud between the owner of the town's only trash dump and the local trash haulers, but never mentions the possible impact on the homeowner's trash bill. The reporter doesn't mention it because he knows that the city council, not the haulers, controls trash rates, and *he* knows that two weeks ago he stated in another story that the city wouldn't pass along the haulers' increased costs to consumers. Think the average reader knows or remembers that?

■ A news report on a local planning agency's meeting is littered with technical expressions that are everyday lingo to the reporter and professional city planners but not to the reader.

■ In one story, the reporter has, somehow, left out the reactions of two key individuals involved. They weren't available for comment, but the reporter didn't mention that; he assumed that fact would be obvious by their absence from the story. The average reader, however, is just as likely to assume that the newspaper is holding back something—intentionally keeping part of the story hidden.

The readership filter works closely with the stance filter (Chapter 1), and these two filters often precede all others. The stance—that assortment of attitudes you employ to collect information—determines how you look for facts; knowing the reader helps you make better choices about how to use the facts you find.

In the same fashion as Rodgers and Wilder, you should play a psychological game with yourself. Obviously, there is no "average" subscriber, especially if you work for a paper that serves a sprawling metropolitan area. You'll have to use your imagination. You'll have to take stock of your paper's circulation and create your version of the fat lady in Kansas City. That doesn't mean you have to write your story in second person, or personalize every paragraph. It simply means you acknowledge that your first obligation is to your reader, not to your editors or to your sources. Pressure of deadlines and absence of sensitivity have eroded that truth in too many newsrooms, so that reporters write without an audience in mind. The nature of the craft leaves little time for questions like, "Why are we doing this?" A readership filter counteracts the pressure.

It's not merely the growing complexity of the world that makes it harder to write. There's also the growing fragmentation of the American readership: your subscriber's increased willingness and ability to seek out specialized publications that appeal to her special interests. The more time she takes for them, the less time she'll spend with you.

The joint forces of the self-help culture and a more economical printing technology have caused a surge of new magazines and newsletters to flood the country. Their focuses are narrow and precise: magazines for organic gardeners, for apartment residents, for owners of home computer systems, for joggers, for riders of certain kinds of motorcycles, for divorced fathers who have custody of their children, for volleyball players—you name it.

This explosion represents a direct challenge to that largest flagbearer of general circulation, the newspaper. Specialized publications can twist reality to meet the expectations and biases of their readers, but newspapers have little such ability.

The competition extends to the individual reporter. Today, more than ever, he faces a heated battle for a subscriber's attention with each story he writes. He needs to use every bit of leverage available to him to make sure the subscriber will read not only the first two paragraphs, but the entire piece.

So be prepared to work at it. Try to figure out how your paper fits into the reader's world. Use your own knowledge of the political and economic makeup of your circulation area; consult your paper's market research department or government agencies; consider, too, precisely when your paper hits the subscriber's porch, and when and where competing media are delivered.

Once you have envisioned your typical subscriber, you can operate with more confidence. As you type the story, your phrasing will be more authoritative, crisper, because you'll be aiming it at a particular individual —not merely putting facts down on paper.

Employing the readership filter is frustrating not only because of the demands it makes, but also because sometimes you simply have to ignore it. Any sensitive reporter knows the feeling of being trapped, obligated by her news values to structure a story in a manner that challenges the reader. She knows the first two paragraphs will probably have to be read a second time in order for the average reader to grasp their complete meaning, but she also knows she has little choice: she just can't make the wording any more accessible without oversimplifying a crucial, complicated fact. Even here, however, the use of the filter is beneficial; it provides something of an objective standard in a painful situation.

To put the filter into practice, here are some of the mental attitudes that should be developed and played off against each other. The reporter should pose them to himself as questions:

What does the reader bring to the story? Remember that most good stories tend to be a series of progressions—over the course of several months, the story may require coverage a dozen times as each new development occurs. Keep in mind an idea of how much of your last story the reader can be expected to retain, and then take advantage of this background by systematically compressing old details.

In each new story, there should be a conscious shift of new elements upward and old ones downward. Segments that had to be explained at length in the first two or three stories should be drastically tightened and moved down. Prod yourself: essence, essence, essence.

Develop strategies—tricks—to accomplish this. One possibility is the use of code words in place of longer phrases or explanations that appeared in previous stories.

For example, when the news first broke, it was reported like this:

> County Assessor Jerome Pierce today was accused of deliberately underappraising a 100-acre parcel owned by the man who is managing his reelection campaign. . . .

Over the next two weeks, there were four follow-up stories in which the charges were gradually verified by the newspaper, so that by the fifth story the lead read:

> The Jerome Pierce appraisal scandal has convinced one-fourth of the county's voters to switch their votes and oppose Pierce's bid for reelection as assessor, a *Tribune* poll shows. . . .

Without that sort of compression of old information, the new material would have to compete for the reader's attention. It should be given easier access.

Other considerations: Is your circulation area homogeneous in terms of income, race, or sociopolitical attitudes? To the extent it is, you can make more valid assumptions—take more risks—about what your "average" reader knows; you can take more for granted. For example, if there is a high ratio of children to total population, you can develop a tendency to pump a little more detail into your education stories.

What is the reader's level of tolerance? In other words, based on the background she brings to the story, what do you have to do to make sure she reads it? How much luxury do you have in constructing your story? How many paragraphs can you take in getting to the essence? What do you have to do to hold the reader's interest once you get it? The variables are different in each story.

Often, however, the answer is mathematical. The smaller you feel the reader's interest in a story will be, the more careful you'll have to be to write tightly and cleanly—explaining the story's impact quickly to convince her to stay with you. Conversely, if you have a story with obvious impact or interest—a 30 percent rise in the crime rate or a woman giving birth to sextuplets—you can relax a little.

What questions will each paragraph trigger? This effort will often avoid a problem we mentioned earlier in this chapter: the story in which the reporter's written logic leaps across several unwritten thoughts—the supporting facts, which the reporter took for granted, much to the dismay of the reader.

Those unintentional voids sometimes do more to provoke disgust and distrust in a reader than anything else. Nobody wants to feel stupid; if a reader can't make sense out of your story, he's going to start reading something else—another story, or perhaps another publication. If it happens too many times, he's going to cancel his subscription.

The readership filter and four other strategies to be described in the following chapters—providing the perspective paragraph, exploiting your inner voice, challenging your creative powers, and editing your copy—are essential refinements that you must add to your bag of mental filters. They provide the polish needed for great writing. They are the filters that enhance the raw, mechanical talent for making the facts fall into place.

5 The Perspective Paragraph

What's wrong with this story?

> SAN DIEGO—The man who became the first person to legally receive Laetrile imports in California is dead just short of his 75th birthday—a victim of the cancer he hoped the drug could halt.
>
> Ray Carnohan of Pacific Beach died of cancer of the pancreas late Saturday, three weeks after winning permission from a federal judge to bring the controversial apricot extract into the United States from Mexico.
>
> He is believed to be the first Californian to have been granted permission to import the substance.
>
> Carnohan, a furniture dealer, had told newsmen. . . .

On and on the story goes, describing Carnohan's motivation for using the drug. Interesting piece, too, except for one chunk of information the reporter knew very well, yet didn't put in the story. It should have followed the second paragraph:

> Laetrile is banned by the federal Food and Drug Administration as ineffective in cancer treatment.

And with that lapse we embark on a little righteous indignation.

The night is dark and the moon is yellow and the leaves come tumbling down and a thousand dead editors break the silence, thrashing with frustration in their graves, still recalling all those otherwise bright reporters who never got the hang of that corny old command, "Tell the reader what it means." Reporters who never could seem to remember to insert that sentence about Laetrile's being illegal—the small fact that would have put the story in focus.

The dead editors howl in unison, demanding an answer for all the times they had to insert a "perspective paragraph" in an otherwise well-written story. Usually, it went just after the first, second, or third paragraph.

Usually, it was merely a dozen or so words that attempted to gently explain the significance of a story in terms of related events or opinions that had been voiced in the past. They plead for an answer, these ghosts, but they'll have to be satisfied with this puny, painful-but-true conclusion: It's much, much easier to write a perspective paragraph than it is to *remember* to write one.

We've reflected several times already on the number of forces and societal changes that buffet a reporter. To guard his sanity, he has to establish some frame of reference, some set of "givens" that hold true in the world. The trouble is that one reporter's given may well be a subscriber's key fact— a piece of information crucial to the reader's full appreciation of a story. The reporter, feeling the information is too obvious to mention, leaves it out.

Which explains why we have conversations like the one you're about to overhear, as the city editor reads the Laetrile death story in its original form, walks over to the reporter who wrote it, and asks him to make the change we suggested:

CITY EDITOR: Say, Jim, you don't explain here specifically that Laetrile is illegal.

REPORTER (with a grimace; it is the third story he has knocked out today):   Aw, everybody knows that.

OR: "Well, the story implies that much."

OR: "Well, hell, we can't spell out *everything*. We have to give the reader some credit."

The comebacks to those three answers are: (1) No, everybody *doesn't* know that. (2) Implication is a game attorneys play. (3) Before we worry about giving the reader some credit, let's concentrate on giving him some help.

To the reporter who wrote the Laetrile story, the illegality of the drug had become a given. For a comparison, think about a citizen drafting a petition demanding clean air. Would she explain how the nose inhales pollution from the atmosphere? In both cases, the writers try to avoid cluttering their stories with facts they consider obvious. In the reporter's case, that produced a mistake.

How can you prevent it? By programming your reporter's mind to be conscious of the need for the perspective paragraph, a device that can lift many a story from average to good or from good to excellent.

The perspective graph (or graphs) is one of the clearest benefits gained from the use of the readership filter discussed in Chapter 4. If you can make yourself conscious of writing for the reader, you are more likely to provide the perspective that is necessary whenever you tell a story to another person—orally or on paper.

As you strengthen the hierarchy of newsthinking habits needed to build your readership filter, you will begin developing a more detailed cluster of skills—another mental filter—specifically tailored to the perspective paragraph.

This perspective filter will force you to ask yourself two more questions each time you prepare a story: (1) Do I need a perspective paragraph and, if so, where should it go? (2) How should I word it? From there, the sequencing and readership filters can be used to write and position the perspective graph.

Good newswriters don't just happen to trip over the element of perspective and luckily kick it into the right place in their stories. They are looking for it; they know its role and the punch it gives their work. Unconsciously, they create the perspective filter, and every story passes through it. If you find yourself lacking that skill, start working on it. Write the word *perspective* on your arm with a felt-tip pen if you have to—anything to jab your memory. By the time the letters fade, the habit will have become ingrained.

What makes the perspective graph such an elusive little devil is the fact that it is often not conspicuous by its absence. For example, a California newspaper's veteran political reporter writes an excellent analysis of the battle between Democratic and Republican gubernatorial candidates for endorsements from organized labor. As far as detail and an explanation of how the labor endorsement process is structured, the article is fine. But it doesn't address the question of what specific benefits candidates receive from a labor endorsement: additional volunteer workers, money, and the precious mention of the candidate's name in the newsletter that the union sends to each member prior to the election.

Obvious? Yes—to the reporter, the candidates he covers, and most union members. But how about the rest of us readers? How about one sentence, three or four paragraphs from the top, beginning something like, "A major labor endorsement usually provides a candidate with. . . ." Hardly too much for a reader to ask, but of course most readers never get a chance to ask or to make suggestions. They must rely on how hard the reporter is willing to work to add an extra dimension to his stories.

Once your mind's perspective filter registers "yes," telling you there's a need, you can choose from a number of methods of inserting the perspective graph. To show you, we will perform minor surgery on several stories, inserting perspective in language that will be underlined. Our aim is not only to illustrate structure, but to emphasize how diligent you have to be. Most of these stories make perfect sense without the perspective graph or phrase. They did not scream for one; the reporters who wrote them had simply gotten into the habit of screaming "Perspective!" at themselves.

1. **Perspective within the lead:** First, the lead with the perspective stripped out:

> Interactive TV is poised to move from regional experiments into living rooms across the nation this year, experts say.
> Products and services that allow consumers to personalize their TV experience will provide much of the buzz at this week's Consumer Electronics Show in Las Vegas. CES will see a raft of announcements by software and hardware suppliers racing to form partnerships and release interactive-TV products.

Now, the lead with perspective:

> <u>Propelled by the coming of digital cable systems</u>, interactive TV is poised to move from regional experiments into living room across the nation this year, experts say.
> Products and services. . . .

Another lead without perspective:

> Former Lincoln Savings & Loan boss Charles H. Keating Jr. pleaded guilty to bankruptcy fraud charges Tuesday.
> In a plea bargain, prosecutors dropped charges that Keating bilked thousands of elderly investors out of their life savings. . . .

With perspective:

> <u>Ending a 10-year battle over the most notorious thrift failure of the 1980s</u>, former Lincoln Savings & Loan boss Charles H. Keating Jr. pleaded guilty to bankruptcy fraud charges Tuesday.
> In a plea bargain, prosecutors dropped charges that. . . .

Without perspective:

> Orthopedic surgeons in Downey say they will stop taking new patients after Sunday.
> The surgeons, who say they will not pay steeply increased malpractice insurance premiums which go into effect Jan. 1, say they will continue to treat patients they are caring for now.
> It remains unclear how many orthopedic surgeons, as well as other doctors in the Southland, will continue to practice medicine after Dec. 31. . . .

With perspective:

> In the first joint action by doctors during the current medical malpractice insurance protest, orthopedic surgeons in Downey say they will stop taking new patients after Sunday.

2. **Perspective directly after the lead.** This is the most common placement because it's easier for the reader to absorb the perspective after he knows the news.

> WASHINGTON—The Administration Tuesday announced its long-expected decision to sell 50 fighter-bombers to Egypt in a Mideast package that includes some of the most sophisticated warplanes in the U.S. arsenal for Saudi Arabia and a sharply reduced supply of planes for Israel.
> It will be the first sale of U.S. warplanes to Egypt.
> Some of the basic decisions in the $4.8 billion sale, which can be blocked by Congress, were made informally months ago, and were no surprise to close observers of U.S. Middle East policy.

> BOSTON—One of City Hall's lengthiest and stormiest battles ended Tuesday with Systems Development Corp. winning a $28.5 million contract to install a modern police emergency communications system.
> The decision ended 20 months of lobbying for the selection of a contractor.
> The City Council voted 10–3 to award the contract to Systems Development. The losing competitor was the Motorola Corp.

> LONDON—An influencial Parliament committee Tuesday called on Britain's Labor government to make drastic cuts in immigration and tighten control of immigrants once they enter Britain.
> The report, written by the House of Commons Select Committee on Race Relations, brought immediate protests from white liberals and immigrant groups.
> It seemed certain to fuel a growing political controversy over non-white immigration, which has stirred increased racial tension in this country.
> The committee said Britain must not continue to allow the high level of non-white immigration of recent years.

3. **Don't be afraid to break up the essence of your story—the first two or three paragraphs—with the insertion of a perspective paragraph.** If you have to sacrifice a little flow for a lot of interpretation, do it and don't sweat about it. That's a classic style-versus-substance confrontation and substance usually deserves to win:

> WASHINGTON—White House and Republican negotiators struggled to narrow their differences over environmental policy and government spending Sunday in an unusual weekend bargaining session to address the final obstacles to agreement on this year's federal budget.
>
> The weekend wrangling represents the stretch drive, not just of the annual budget battle, but of the entire tumultuous year of Congress, which began with the grand drama of President Clinton's impeachment trial and is ending in bitter jockeying over relatively small budget differences. Republican leaders are hoping to settle the handful of environmental, education and law enforcement disputes and pass the budget in time for Congress to adjourn for the year by midweek.
>
> To that end, GOP negotiators were hoping to wrap up negotiations on the Interior Department budget as early as today. But that will require them to resolve such contentious issues as the funding Clinton is seeking to acquire environmentally sensitive land and policy changes the administration believes would weaken regulation of mining, oil, and other industries.
>
> "We've made some progress, but we're not there yet," said Sen. Slade Gorton (R-Wash.), the GOP's lead negotiator on environmental issues, after a session in which Republicans offered to provide $335 million more for the Interior Department and related agencies than the $14.5 billion they had offered earlier.

On the other hand, don't be surprised to find new factors that make it worthwhile to delay the perspective graph. Perhaps you have a particularly good quote that develops your story's essence, and the perspective paragraph you want to use is more obligatory than crucial. Similarly, your perspective material may be too wordy to form a dependent clause in the lead, and may require the contextual support of the first two to four paragraphs of the story. Like this:

> MUSCATINE, Iowa—Rosa Mendoza, who heads the multicultural center in this fading "Pearl of the Mississippi" known for a Heinz ketchup factory and little else, used to have a hard time commanding the attention of elected officials.

Nowadays, Mendoza can't get two of the most powerful men in America, George W. Bush and Al Gore, off the phone. Their presidential campaigns want her help in Muscatine and won't seem to take no for an answer.

"They're calling me all the time, telling me they need me to take part in this event or that event, join this committee or that committee," a bemused Mendoza said. "It's sad, really, because these politicians never seemed to care about our problems before. But, hey, we Hispanics need to take advantage of this."

Improbable as it sounds, Iowa, with only 56,000 Latinos statewide, has become an early testing ground for the national strategies Gore and Bush are formulating to capture Latino votes—and the support of community activists such as Mendoza.

The early effort reflects the increasingly active and influential role of Latino voters, particularly in states key to the presidential election, such as California, Texas, and New York.

The embrace of Latinos in Iowa carries a symbolic message too. It allows Bush and Gore to package themselves as the candidates of choice for non-Latino voters looking for more inclusive, softer-edged candidates.

4. **Placing the perspective several graphs down is often done in follow-up stories on which the background is relatively well known.** This technique was touched on in Chapter 4: With each new progression in a developing story, move the old-but-vital information down and the new material up.

An initiative campaign asking city voters to eliminate the "living wage" section of the city charter has failed by a big margin, officials said Tuesday.

Councilman Ralph Rogers, the leader of the campaign to put the issue on the June primary election ballot, conceded that "apparently we have failed" to gather sufficient signatures, but said he would continue to work to get the proposal on the ballot in November.

The secretary of the County Federation of Labor, Earvin Getty, criticized Rogers for waging "a campaign against the working poor" that was financed by big business and kept moving with the aid of paid petition circulators. Getty complained at a news conference that Rogers had tried to mislead the public by calling his effort an effort to cut "bloated municipal spending."

The living wage section of the city charter, approved by voters in 1997, requires that city contractors pay their employees at least $7.85 an hour plus insurance benefits—effectively about three dollars an hour above the minimum wage. Analysts say it has boosted the wages of 5,000 low-income employees, primarily those who work at Springfield International Airport.

Think about how many times you've seen a story like the previous one made ponderous by the placement of the perspective paragraph directly after the lead. There's no reason for it. It's the kind of story that must have been in the news for months. You still need to explain this kind of story to those readers who haven't been exposed to it or have forgotten about it, but because of your previous coverage, the number of such readers has dwindled. Take advantage of that.

In newly breaking stories, however, feel free to string several perspective paragraphs together high up in the story. You're not blocking the reader from the news—you're merely reacting to the fact that sometimes it's harder to explain the significance of an event than the essence of it. Example:

Across the South, a series of unresolved, racially motivated killings of blacks from the civil rights era are under new scrutiny. Among them: the 1963 racist bombing that killed four black girls in a downtown Birmingham church.

This fresh round of investigations into the long-ago killings, many of which were ignored by the authorities for years, was inspired by the well-publicized conviction in 1994 of an aging white defendant in the 1963 assassination of the Mississippi civil rights leader Medgar Evers.

For years, black community leaders and relatives of victims complained about the lack of action in both the more-prominent and lesser-known cases. But their urgings have been taken more seriously recently, experts and historians say, because the political, social, and legal climate in the South has changed so significantly since the killings.

Blacks have steadily gained political power and have pushed for these cases to be heard before today's racially diverse juries. At the same time, more witnesses, perhaps with less fear of retaliation and with heavy consciences they want to unburden, are coming forward. And a new breed of prosecutors and investigators, feeling a sense of urgency as many witnesses and defendants in the cases grow old, is realizing the important role that resolving these cases can play in the South's efforts to move beyond its past of racial hate and terrorism.

At least seven long-dormant cases are now being re-examined in the South. A few are before grand juries or are being prosecuted. But some have only just begun to be reinvestigated and have had little national attention. There is the little-known case of the 1967 car-bombing of a black father of five who had been promoted to chemical mixer in a factory, a job usually re-served for white men. Another example of a lesser-known case involved the 1967 shooting of a black man at a protest by black university students.

The officials pursuing these cases are mostly Southern and white. Most are . . .

5. **Make sure your reflex in favor of perspective doesn't make the story unreadable.** Consider this:

> <u>Attempting to duplicate last year's legislation that required any San Fernando Valley secession effort to go before Los Angeles voters citywide,</u> a state lawmaker plans to introduce a bill that would require a districtwide vote for any effort to carve up the Los Angeles Unified School District.
>
> The bill, to be carried by Assemblyman Tony Cardenas (D-Sylmar) at the request of the teachers union, would significantly hamper the efforts of San Fernando Valley groups trying to break away from the giant LAUSD.
>
> Cardenas said his proposal "would apply . . .

Now, the dependent clause the reporter used to provide perspective measured 21 words—nearly half of the length of the sentence itself. The lesson is that sometimes you have to choose between news and perspective when the perspective is complex. In this case, the writer should have bumped down the perspective so that the story read:

> A state lawmaker plans to introduce a bill that would re-quire a districtwide vote for any effort to carve up the Los Angeles Unified School District.
>
> The bill, to be carried by Assemblyman Tony Cardenas (D-Sylmar) at the request of the teachers union, would significantly hamper the efforts of San Fernando Valley groups trying to break away from the giant LAUSD.
>
> <u>The bill echoes legislation passed last year in which law-makers required a citywide vote in order for the San Fernando Valley to secede from the City of Los Angeles.</u>
>
> Cardenas said his proposal "would apply . . .

It's the kind of trade-off you'll find yourself making as your reporter's mind searches for the perspective in every story you write. The better you get at looking, the more structural problems you'll create for yourself. You'll have to be tough. Are you going to remember that need for balance, or are you going to be overcome by the opportunity to cram all your newfound perspective into the first paragraph, damn the readability and full speed ahead?

The ghosts of a thousand dead editors would appreciate an answer.

More on "The Perspective Paragraph" in the Appendix:

- How the WTO protest in Seattle taxed some writers' use of perspective

CHAPTER

6

Your Inner Voice

And so the story is being written. The lead has been perfected, the sequence has been carved out. The other filters—memory, readership, and perspective—have received the appropriate attention. The words can begin to flow.

But as they do, yet another important stage takes place, one that heavily influences the impact of the writer's words and her ability to string those words together in a variety of styles. To illustrate it, let's revisit Ms. Turner, whom we last saw in Chapter 3 demonstrating the use of our lead filter. It's Monday afternoon in the newsroom and she's working, a bit leisurely, on a feature about an uneducated but well-read 84-year-old man who wrote a 400-year genealogical history of his family.

She writes slowly, toying with the words:

> When had the idea of chasing centuries of his family's history popped into the old man's head? John Bowman could only guess. Twenty years ago, perhaps, after he had retired; one of his sons had given him what was supposed to be a family crest.
>
> "That got me thinking," he said.
>
> He thought of the stories he could tell—of sailing from St. Louis to India in 1917 on an engineering job; marrying the teenage daughter of an officer in the British occupying force; returning to America a decade later with a small fortune, only to lose it in the Depression; and, finally, settling in Boston, expanding the family and building a business.
>
> And there were the tantalizing stories his father had told him—about a Dutch mercenary who went to England to fight for King Henry VIII; about the mercenary's grandson who sailed to America as an indentured servant and changed his name to Bowman, a tribute to the family's tradition of skill with the bow and arrow; and about the generations that followed during the next 300 years.

John Bowman knew he was in the middle of all those stories, but he did not know quite what to do with them. An inveterate collector, he had saved scores of family documents, pictures, and memories. But for decades their importance merely germinated—until a year ago.

It was then, at the age of 83 and with a fifth-grade education, that Bowman began trying to sort out the family's legends and history.

The result was a surprisingly polished 122-page genealogical history. . . .

Suddenly, there's a tap on her shoulder from her city editor. There's been a bad traffic accident with some odd complications. Since Turner isn't on deadline, could she work it as a quick daily for tomorrow morning's paper?

Ninety minutes later, the story is out of her typewriter. It begins:

A weekend reunion in Baja California for three men who grew up together in Santa Ana turned to tragedy after a car accident killed one and injured the others.

Before the weekend was over, one of them was forced to wait nearly a day and pay nearly $11,000 so he could get treatment at a U.S. hospital. The other was put in a jail cell, then hospitalized under police guard so he could be questioned.

On Monday, Barry Patrick Walshe, 31, of Newport Beach, was in a Tijuana hospital under orders of authorities in Rosarito Beach, where the single-car accident occurred Sunday, said Tijuana police spokesman Raul Gonsalez.

Think about it: Compassionate, sensitive, measured phrasing one moment, and crisp urgency the next. Why, it's a marvel, to be able to switch styles of writing like that. Oh, to be blessed with such talent. . . .

Ah, but being blessed with talent is hardly the complete explanation. Consider hard work. And imagination. And, finally, consider another mental filter, this one aimed at the delicate artistry of the inner voice—the strategies a writer uses to convert his or her thought impulses into words through silent speech. It seems to be a process all writers use, but with widely differing degrees of consciousness and risk.

Depending on the kind of writing you do, paying increased attention to your inner voice can make you more aware of how you shape the wording of your story. With that awareness, you can try to exercise more control over the tone of the inner voice in order to increase the diversity of your writing approaches.

What Ms. Turner did was abandon her everyday inner voice—the one she uses to talk to herself about such mundane matters as the grocery list—and consciously take inventory of the writing voices she has built up over the years. Did the story deserve a touch of awe? Lightheartedness? Sarcasm? Aggressiveness? Sometimes she can verbally describe the emotion or tone she is trying to inject; other times, she merely feels the urge to give the story a certain flavor—she can't say exactly what, but she knows the style she's searching for.

Finally, she made her choices. For the Bowman feature, she would compose in a leisurely, expansive voice, a voice suited to the sweeping nature of the man's accomplishment. He had sifted through history, and now so would she. For the traffic accident story, the choice was easier. She needed a voice of urgency, one that could tell a story with the proper mixture of terseness and drama dominated by the chronology of the event. A no-frills flight.

Through these maneuvers, Turner assumed her writing stance—a process similar to the prewriting, information-gathering stance we examined in Chapter 1. Here she created a filter to help deflect inappropriate impulses and prod her writing in the proper direction. Once again, she was responding to the peculiar nature of the job of newspaper reporter—particularly the task of general assignment reporter—and the flexibility it demands.

Look at it this way. If you're Maureen Dowd, and your prime concern is your *New York Times* column, your writing will be formed by a consistent inner voice; the column, after all, is intended to allow a writer with a relatively fixed point of view to interpret patterns of events. On general assignment it's almost completely reversed; you must cope with an unpredictable variety of assignments that require you to tell stories in any number of ways. Thus it will not be merely the order in which you put your paragraphs together that determines how well you succeed. You must also be sure to select the tone of writing that best tells the story and best exploits its elements.

You do that through consciously adopting a particular tone of inner voice to compose the story—to translate your thoughts to the computer screen. Concentrate on this technique in order to take advantage of the power words seem to gain when the writer composes in a strong, confident inner voice and then transmits that force—as if it moved from his brain through his fingers—onto the page.

The more conscious you are of the technique, the more effective you will be in meeting the challenge of a story that calls for a precise style—

sensitive, bold, urgent, authoritative, or any of a dozen others. Those kinds of qualities will help almost any story as long as the correct dosage is administered.

Remember the concept of translation. It is a process a good newswriter engages in several times during the course of a story. The initial stage, which we viewed in the sequencing process (Chapter 3), involves translating the observed order of events into an order that brings out the story's essence. A second stage of translation occurs when the reporter reworks the technical or awkward phrases used by his sources (excluding quotations), putting the words into understandable English. In both of these cases, a reporter can get away with far less than the maximum effort, and few editors will notice. It's the writer's intensity—his pride in craftsmanship—that determines whether and how thoroughly the translation will be made.

Further translation occurs as the reporter outlines his story. And even if he makes the right organizational choices, he must continue to concentrate to ensure their translation onto the screen. If he types too casually, believing the story will simply "flow," he may butcher the literacy and smooth sequence that he painstakingly created in his outline.

With this in mind, the skilled reporter learns to add an inner voice filter to his newswriting. He takes a moment to consider what kind of translation mechanism is needed to communicate the story, most of which still remains in his head. Before he begins composing, he poses the question, "What kind of inner voice should I use to bring this story to life?"

He has to make the right kind of choice; an inappropriate one can ruin a story, no matter how talented the writer is. If, for example, he adopts a slashing, staccato delivery for a soft feature piece about an elderly nun's last day teaching Catholic school, there may be no hope for him.

Some writers may quarrel with delving into specific styles of inner voice; they may feel it implies a coldly calculated approach to a skill which, after all, is considered an art—especially by people who are good at it. And yet, if you follow a good newswriter's work over the months, you will be able to see that he intentionally changes his style depending on the type of story. The rhythms of sentence structure vary, the urgency of tone isn't always the same, the level of aggressiveness rises or falls. The writer in question may not be aware—or may not admit—that he has built a repertoire of inner voices, but he has. He has also built a parallel skill that is just as important: the ability to match the correct inner voice to each story, or to invent new ones.

For example, if we press Ms. Turner about how she handled the traffic story, we can drag this confession out of her: "Well," she says, "I have this game I play with myself whenever I have to compress a bunch of facts on deadline. I try to make it sound like [television anchorman] Peter Jennings— I imagine that he's reading the final version on the air. First, I read through the material I have to work with, and then I compose in his voice. I'm trying to get the feeling of typing the words as though I were transcribing his version. Why does it work? I guess because I'm used to the rhythm of his writing—I watch his show a lot—and because his style is suited perfectly to that kind of job, where you have to make sense of a complex story within the limitations of TV airtime. He's great. That's why I steal from him, if you want to call it that."

My suggestion here is not that you concentrate on stealing other writers' styles, but that you take pains to first assert your own inner voice—a standard tone—and then develop a variety of supplementary voices.

When an editor works with a writer for a while, he grows familiar with the writer's inner voice(s), and begins to "hear" the story as he copyedits it. He becomes used to the better writers' ability to inject a great range of emotion, tone, and pacing into their work. And he plods through the dullness of his less-inspired reporters, who seem to write with few peaks or valleys in their construction. But sometimes, to the editor's surprise, a reporter with a normally dull style produces an inspired piece. In the words of the delighted wife whose bumbling husband finally cooked a perfect, medium-rare roast beef, "What went wrong?"

If you assume that the subject matter somehow lit a fire under the reporter, your assumption is too broad. A stage in between is the real key. Yes, the subject did inspire the reporter—enough to finally make him *concentrate* on translating the force of what he felt to the screen. Countless other times, that reporter had been inspired by his material, but had not been able to express that inspiration. He had not concentrated hard enough on translating those perceptions, filtering them through his inner voice. When he composed his story the feelings weren't communicated. A reporter more conscious of pulling those feelings out and putting them on the line would have done far better in similar circumstances.

And so I speak to the introverts in the audience: There are many ways to enjoy a civilized life while keeping your feelings hidden—but not at the keyboard. You cannot wait for dramatic events to force you to express those feelings. That will improve your writing only in a smattering of cases. You have to work on bringing your thoughts out of your gut. The color, the sparkle, the liveliness that make good writing—they lie there.

We're not talking about altering the facts, or sacrificing basic objectivity. We're talking about the ability to write about a war-torn port, full of sunken ships and collapsed piers, as "a smoking vision of hell." We're talking about a mobster's Cadillac that "gleamed like a huge, blue steel egg." We're talking about being able to share our inner visions. Let your inner voice be the spot where the icy orderliness of rationality and the uncontrollable blaze of emotion come together, shaping your composition.

Consider a typical textbook description of how thought impulses are crystallized into words. It roughly duplicates the process a reporter goes through in building his story framework and then his outline, narrowing his focus until he begins writing.

The first phase in this four-step thought-to-speech process is a state of awareness. Its contents cannot be specified; at the most, we have only a vague outline of thought. Then:

1. The awareness hardens into crude ideas that form the general scheme of thought. Some animals may communicate when thought reaches this crude level, but we humans are more sophisticated; we do not yet speak. The thoughts are not sufficiently explicit to permit verbal expression.
2. The scheme of thought activates a grammatical scheme. Thought becomes further focused, until it is like the linear pattern into which the stones of a mosaic (the words) are to be fitted.
3. In the final phase, we make the choice of the appropriate words—the filling in of the design.

Be conscious of the unity among those stages. When a good newswriter begins working on a story, he is launching a mental process aimed at forming a pattern into which words can be laid. Every step he takes determines how accurate the pattern will be; every step influences the next step. The scope of your research influences your ability to construct a good outline, and the strength and logic of that outline influence the ease with which you can translate your thoughts into a literate story. Each link in the chain of thought must be secure.

Then—and only then—you can flick a mental trigger and begin composing a story that meets your true potential. Give your inner voice weak material to work with and it will produce eloquent pap. But give a well-planned, logical story outline to a surging inner voice and the magic begins to happen. The two forces build on each other; the words are dazzling. This is the end of a long process of crystallization. A crude idea—a story angle—has been refined, time and again. Its words carry a power no one had anticipated, and when they reach the newspaper subscriber, they initiate another chain of energy. They begin making him think about the issue in question, setting off new ideas in his mind, until he begins a crystallizing process of his own, using the story to obtain a clearer perspective of his world.

Rarely are you lucky enough to see the steps merge, but you must believe they can. Whatever inner voice you choose to compose in, give it the spirit to transcend the moment; make it a voice that believes in what it is saying.

Conscious use of the inner voice can expand the writer's creativity. When he is pondering the phrasing of a story, he can try composing it in several different styles of inner voice, comparing the results in his mind. Experimenting this way avoids the slight inhibition that crops up whenever a writer types his initial impulses. The inner voice can run through a series of styles, and the reporter can listen. He can pick the approach and phrasing he wants, and then make the translation to paper. As he does, yet another filter—the stuff of genius—comes into play. Let us pursue it.

More on "Your Inner Voice" in the Appendix:

- The voice behind a news analysis

7 Tapping the Right Brain

*The subjective must take back the world from the objective
gorillas and guerillas of the world. . . .*
—Lawrence Ferlinghetti, San Francisco poet

In the next two chapters we are going to look at your newswriting in the context of a commonly discussed creature called creativity and a popular but still-misunderstood neurological principle called "the right brain." Because your creative powers appear to be centered in the right side of the brain, we'll examine the brain issues in this chapter and discuss creative attitudes in Chapter 8. Together, the two chapters produce the background for the development of a creativity filter. Now let's get back to the newsroom, where we overhear a reporter making a common complaint to an editor.

The reporter is having a hard time doing justice to a potentially good feature story about a child stricken with leukemia holding on to life. When the boy was two, his parents were told he had six months to live. Now he is five—alive because of a series of surprising remissions. The parents are delighted and yet weary of the strain. The reporter, having interviewed them and the child, is weary, too.

". . . and so what's happened is that I'm dried up," he tells his editor. "You had me working four straight months on that damn political coverage, and it soured me. All that structured stuff, I just don't feel like I can turn on my creative juices anymore—even with a piece like this one."

Most newspaper editors pride themselves on the ability to resolve a sensitive conflict like that with the reply, "Tough," or, "Just let the story tell itself." It's hard to blame them; there simply isn't time to sit down and say to the reporter, "Look. Eastern cultures believe strongly in utilizing the subconscious, spiritual part of yourself to capture ideas that the day-to-day part of your mind omits or can't dig up. So I'd appreciate it if you'd concentrate on using that part—your subconscious, your subjective side—when you find yourself doing a feature or creative assignment."

Yet there is a compromise explanation—a way of looking at things—that any editor or reporter should consider when the creative fountain seems to run dry, when the writer needs to have faith in his ability to find a solution to a tough story. It lies in understanding and then exploiting the scientific principle that a full half of your brain is reserved for the kind of thinking that produces creative newswriting. The right cerebral hemisphere—the right side of the brain—performs the creative work of your mind. By playing a series of mind games with yourself—and particularly by adopting a style of outlining that is tailored to your brain's creative bent—you can more successfully tap that inherent creativity. First, however, let's lay the groundwork.

Experiments have shown that the right brain thinks, for the most part, in ways that its owner cannot verbalize. The artistic, creative impulses you feel when ideas suddenly fall into place are produced by the right hemisphere. When it is time for your mind to put a collection of concepts, symbols, or emotions into perspective—to glean some emotional truth from a bunch of jumbled elements—it is your right brain that goes to work.

The impulses that produce poetry and music originate on this side of the brain. So does intuition. So does the ability to perceive spatial relationships, such as the ballet dancer's uncanny ability to maneuver between two partners, leaping and twisting through a small opening without colliding with anyone.

The left cerebral hemisphere, meanwhile, is responsible for carrying out the better-known, "rational" functions of everyday life. It deals with step-by-step arrangement of words, numbers, and intellectual tasks. It thinks in sequential patterns. The work of mastering speech, arithmetic, and logic goes on here. The mental work of, say, a Marine drill sergeant—or anyone else who concentrates on going by the book—is primarily dependent on the left brain, too.

The right and left sides work together, and we are never conscious of the complex, sometimes mysterious cross-talk that goes on between the two halves. Yet it is the precision of this communication between the two sides that seems to determine how well a reporter handles thousands of maneuvers that call for him to balance and alternate quickly between his logical and emotional talents.

Let's consider an isolated process, speech, which is usually the domain of the left cerebral hemisphere. Remember the leukemia story? You're trying to tell the editor that the boy's battle will be a good story because it illustrates both exceptional courage and agony. Your ability to appreciate that concept is developed in your right brain. But the right brain has only the simplest verbal skills; it cannot express that appreciation. So the impulse is fed to the left brain, whose neuronal structure is more directly hooked up to the human speech system. Out comes your explanation.

In interviewing or writing, the key is often the ability to merge a hard, cold instinct for facts with a sensitive manner. The most interesting writers seem to be better at merging the two sides of their brains than the rest of us. With no specialized training, they have developed the most precise methods of exploiting their right-brain talents. They know when to push themselves for a creative solution and when to stop pushing—when to wait and let their unconscious, subjective side do the work. They have a strong, inexplicable belief that the proper impulses and flashes will bubble to the top.

When they need inspiration, when they need that unique feature angle that just won't seem to come, they instinctively turn the job over to their creativity filter, which is housed in the right brain. The right brain won't put the story into words for them—it probably can't. Instead, it will explore the story in a deeper fashion. It will look for the parts and the wholes—the relationships between the facts and the story's essence.

Your left brain may be counting the trees; your right brain is concentrating on the forest, examining how the trees fit in. Your left brain may be thinking that the leukemia victim has lived two and a half years longer than the doctors had predicted; your right brain is asking questions like, "How does this event relate to contemporary medicine, the family's expectations, the boy's emotions?" Your left brain looks at how things are; your right brain wonders how else they might be. The right brain rummages through dozens of possible combinations of facts, always with an aesthetic sense, a desire to make things fit.

Do you know the feeling of being so engrossed in your work that time stands still? That everything around you—noises, voices, movement—is shut out? When you sense all the pieces of a story falling into place? When something inside you says, "Hold on, that's it!"? In those moments, the right half of your brain has taken charge. You have stepped outside the narrow, left-brain way of looking at things—one piece of information after another—and are now working at a different level of consciousness, a state of mind in which you expose your information not merely to your intellectual depth as a reporter but to your emotional depth as a human being. You must develop the confidence to shift into this way of thinking so that you can sufficiently "play" with the facts you've gathered, shifting them around in your head, knowing that when you find the right combination a spark will go off inside you.

The right-brain theory was just poking its head into popular culture when I first wrote this book. Soon, in fields like education, business management, and medicine, a wave of specialists, conferences, and books on the subject sprouted. To this day they begin by describing how the right brain works, and then insisting that once you're aware of the left-right relationship, you can benefit from it.

The best example of how to teach yourself to consciously make use of the right-brain concept is contained in *Drawing on the Right Side of the Brain* by Betty Edwards, an art instructor who began tailoring her instruction to right-brain ways of thinking in the 1960s. She explains to her students how the left brain's sequential and verbal biases make it difficult for the average person to liberate his artistic impulses, and then tries to teach them how to experience the shift into a "right-mode stage of consciousness." She wants them to force themselves to stop thinking in words and to concentrate on letting the visual images in their minds slide directly onto the blank sheet of paper, not allowing the left brain's verbal interpretation of the image to get in the way.

There is often a peculiar feeling when one tries to shut off the left brain (an act that's virtually impossible, scientifically speaking, but don't let that stop you; it's more important to imagine that a pure right-brain stream of thought is achievable). See if Edwards's anecdote sounds familiar:

> One artist told me, "When I'm really working well, it's like nothing else I've ever experienced. I feel at *one* with the work; the painter, the painting, it's all one. I feel excited, but calm—exhilarated, but in full control. It's not exactly happiness; it's more like bliss; I think it's what keeps me coming back and back to painting and drawing."
>
> In art, the right-brain concept leads to techniques such as using "negative space," drawing with most attention paid to the white shapes that develop between the artwork and the edge of the paper as the drawing progresses. Again, the intent is to break the would-be artist away from his left brain's fixation with literally interpreting the object that is being drawn.

"The negative spaces, bounded by the format, require the same degree of attention and care that the positive forms require," Edwards says. "Beginning students generally lavish all their attention on the objects, persons or forms in their drawings, and then sort of 'fill in the background.'

"It may seem hard to believe at this moment," she tells her new students, "but if care and attention are lavished on the negative spaces, the forms will take care of themselves."

In newswriting, the right-brain concept fits snugly into the process all writers go through. They search their minds for an "angle"—an emotional impulse, a direction, a flash. Often it's a feeling they can't put into words, but it gives them the first clue about how to tell a story. That's the right side at work.

From there, they begin finding words to fit into that concept (left brain). As the story develops, they look for other subangles, other twists (right brain). When they find them, they return to the process of phrasing (left brain).

Over and over, the unconscious shift happens. The right cerebral hemisphere produces the creative impulse that sends you in the proper direction; the left hemisphere performs the equally complex chore of putting the words and graphs into a precise sequence.

Okay, that's theory. How do you make it come alive? How can you heighten it? One of the best and easiest techniques is to adopt a style of outlining that forces your right brain to go to work, a style that tries to shut off the sequential side of your mind and liberate the other. This is an interim step. It should occur between the time you begin to feel a vague sequence develop and the time you prepare a standard, graph-by-graph, vertical outline of your story.

First, take an unlined piece of paper (lines might put your mind in a step-after-step, left-brain framework). Draw a circle in the center of the page, and inside the circle write a word—a slug—that best defines the story's central theme. Next, as soon as any related concept, issue, point, or feeling in the story strikes you, write a one-word symbol for it somewhere else on the paper. Draw a circle around that word and draw a line connecting it to the main circle. Just wait for the feelings to arise, and then mark them down wherever they seem to fit—above, below, or off to the side of the main circle. You're creating an outline that lets the components float in space, giving you a better chance to visualize the many relationships between them.

Diagram 7.1 is an example of what a simplified right-brain outline of the leukemia story might look like. If you study this kind of outline while you mull over a more formal sequence, it will become easier to find an angle that goes beyond the straight facts, so that you don't have to settle for dull, everyday approaches like:

> A 5-year-old boy has won a 3-year struggle with leukemia despite his doctors' predictions that he would live only 6 months.
> The parents of Darnell Thomas say they are . . .

Let's examine a right-brain outline of a far more complex story—a news analysis of a Philadelphia program that had dramatically cut the number of street gang deaths. The story was tricky not merely because it combined statistics, politics, bureaucracy, and atmosphere, but because it was being written for a Los Angeles newspaper. It attempted to contrast Philadelphia's success with Los Angeles's failure in controlling street gang violence. Thus in composing it, the reporter had to bounce a succession of

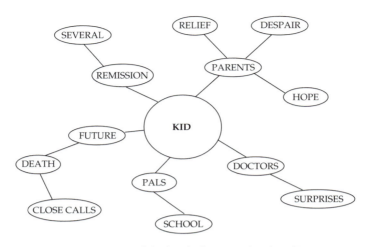

DIAGRAM 7.1   A simplified right-brain style of outline.

variables off each other quickly—first, an anecdote that illustrated Philadelphia's problem, followed by a statistical summary of Philadelphia's success; then, to provide the article's perspective, a summary of Los Angeles's problem with controlling gangs, and Los Angeles's voids; then back to a capsule description of how Philadelphia's program worked.

The reporter knew that unless he handled these elements with great coordination, the reader might need to read ten or fifteen paragraphs to gain the required base of knowledge. Like a motion picture director who senses his audience won't sit through fifteen diverse, unrelated "establishing" shots at the beginning of a film, the reporter had to put a premium on streamlining—something he could achieve only by organization. In Diagram 7.2, you can see the number of tentacles that flow from the reporter's central concept, "CRISIS."

Only after the reporter had allowed his story elements to "float" was he ready to work on a sequential outline. He first had to give his mind a chance to examine the periphery of the story as well as the center. He had to look for the pieces that best exploited the essence of the story, the ones that would make the reader feel the way he felt. He needed to look for something—some conversation, some quote, some gesture—that defined the story. Ironically, in this case the effort was unsuccessful. The reporter (yours truly) was unable to overcome the burden of presenting the statistical information, and the story appeared in a dry, factual style. But he knew he had pushed his creative faculties as hard as he could, and so he was satisfied, even though he had failed to achieve his ultimate goal.

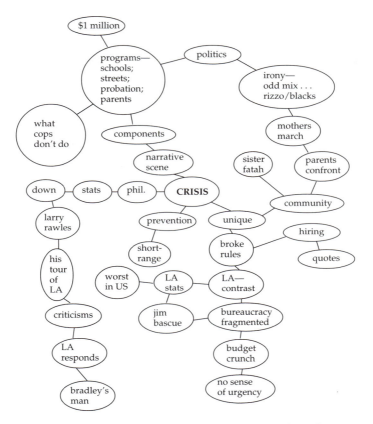

DIAGRAM 7.2   A more complex story as seen by the right brain.

Within the right-brain theory is an intriguing explanation of why some types of thoughts are so difficult to verbalize, and why some people camouflage right-brain motives with left-brain rationalizations. This concept is interesting because as we mature we are usually confronted with an increasing number of impulses that seem too complex for words, and yet have to be acted on. Personally and professionally it's the same:

1.   An editor is shown a picture of a celebrity making an obscene gesture. He cringes and says, "OK, run it—but no bigger than two columns." Later, when his boss compliments him on his restraint, the editor may try to describe his rationale, but what he really did at the time was to subconsciously envision the tolerable level: how big the picture could be run to exploit its value without offending too many sensibilities.

At the moment he made the decision, he was acting on instinct. Two columns just felt right—again, the right brain at work. Of course, editors and their bosses don't like to admit they run on such impulses—it sounds too chaotic, too unbusinesslike—so we usually hear other, more elaborate, left-brain explanations. Instinct? They don't often promote you for your instinct.

2. A couple finds a new apartment. All he emphasizes is the fact that it's smaller than their current apartment. The first thing that strikes her is its charm, the way the rooms are arranged, the angle of the cathedral ceilings. It just feels right.

The point: That "feel" has just as much intelligence behind it—was produced by the same electrochemical transmission in the brain—as the spoken reaction of the man who says, "It's too small." The couple will have to argue the point, just as your own right and left hemispheres argue and then merge when the brain is called on to process information.

Writers should understand this process not simply to improve the management of their information, but also to help them deal with the often contradictory swirl of people they confront in their jobs. Can a successful young jockey really express why he is so much better than his competitors? Within himself he may feel confident of his uncommon ability to sense a horse's instincts and to respond perfectly to those cues—but such perceptions are ordinarily controlled by the right brain. Can they truly be translated into a language that the left brain can express?

Or can a baseball player who hit a game-winning home run really answer the standard question, "What were you thinking about when you hit it?" Athletes suffer from a reputation for dumbness for giving stock answers to such questions, but it is not their fault that they cannot explain such things. Their skills are buried in a right-brain sense of physical unity, a feeling that usually defies verbalization. A hundred physical and emotional variables come together inside the batter at the moment the pitcher releases the ball. The right variables plus the right pitch equal a home run.

Suppose when you were a child in school, your teacher had talked to the class about the importance of feelings that cannot be expressed as words. Suppose you had somehow avoided the habit of assuming that you'd won an argument whenever your rival became tongue-tied. Suppose you'd never grown used to assuming, "Ah-ha! I've beaten him; he's at a loss for words. He's run out of valid thoughts." Remember, there is a profound but mute intelligence at work in the right brain. The fact that an impulse does not cross over to the left half, where it can be routed to the speech center, does not dim its merit. Nevertheless, our culture employs its prejudice of taking no one seriously unless he can express himself in conventional speech (or establish himself as a genius in some other medium). A kid can't talk very intelligibly or intelligently, so he's rejected as "dumb." But wait—the same kid is a marvelous guitar player. He can hear you hum a complicated melody and duplicate it immediately on his instrument. Arrangement of words is a left-brain talent; the confluence of musical notes is a right-brain talent. Who's dumb?

This is not a plea to regard everyone as intelligent, or to believe that everyone has the potential to offer equally intelligent ideas. Certainly, you have had—and will continue to have—interviewing experiences or phone conversations with people who are wrong, stupid, inaccurate, unimportant, or all of the above. The key is to not tune them out immediately just because they *seem* that way.

The next time you encounter a person like that in your reporting, give him a chance in the context of right-brain talents. Give him the benefit of the doubt. Allow for the possibility that something important is being produced by his mind, and perhaps he simply can't get it out without help from the interviewer.

Think about the past. How much have you missed by not being more sensitive, by not recognizing that this person's thoughts could be as eloquent or as significant or as quotable as anyone else's, if only somebody—you—could make the effort to help him pull those thoughts out?

We can't predict such circumstances or solutions. But the next time you're faced with a situation in which a potentially good topic is being drowned by an inarticulate or uncommunicative subject, consider the possibility that he is holding back against his will. Try asking something absurdly obvious like, "Are you having trouble talking about this?" or "What do you find hardest to talk about?" Then ask why. Those questions may tap some hidden flow of words on some other channel, and who knows what you'll get?

Rest assured, you will waste time this way. But just as certainly—although far less predictably—you'll find information or emotion that will improve your story, or possibly lead you to another one. That's what the game is about, isn't it?

Enough philosophizing. Let's get back to the newsroom.

More on "Tapping the Right Brain" in the Appendix:

■ Techniques for injecting the "emotional truth" into your writing

CHAPTER
8 Creativity

Are you growing tired of hearing our Ms. Turner praised to the skies? Well, the people who work with Turner get a little sick of her, too. She perplexes them. "Why," they ask themselves over that second beer at the end of the day, "is she the one who *unfailingly* comes up with the brilliant story idea or the unique angle? Why is she the one whose writing always seems to run in directions no one can anticipate?" There is no predictable style to her work, except that it seems to weave perception, logic, and surprise in an endless stream.

"Why," her colleagues groan, waiting for the third round to arrive, "is she *different* from the rest?" How does she do it? Can they ever know? She seems to revel in the mystique of her talent, to delight in somehow letting the story control her as much as she controls it.

We say such reporters are creative. We envy them and we can't help being jealous. But we rarely stop to try to compare Ms. Turner's mental processes or output with our own, to see where our deficiencies may lie. When we do, we find that she has translated what are normally interpreted as personality traits into simple work habits. Magic? There is none. Her creativity is easily liberated because she has the discipline to take on challenging topics and the organizational skills to handle them. Her creativity filter reminds her not only to use strategies like right-brain outlining (as described in Chapter 7), but also to constantly test her free-flowing creative impulses with a long list of questions. To the degree that she wishes to toy with a story—to take chances, to take risks—she must also firm up her methodology to make sure those creative impulses are pushed in the right direction.

There is a lot of unseen pain in this. Turner rarely feels completely satisfied; there are always new plateaus for her creative energies to reach. That is one of her demons—the tension that builds when her subconscious begins to prod her. The moment, for example, when she recognizes a story that should be written, and knows that it will be a frustrating pursuit. It is the type of story no one else will go after; she could avoid it without worrying about the competition. She hates the idea of doing it and yet she hates the idea of not doing it. She feels anxious, alone, worried by the possibility that

69

she is venturing into lost territory. If no one else has yet written such a story, if no one else is interested now, perhaps it isn't a valid topic. Yet she also feels driven by a great sense of urgency. She is torn, knowing that ultimately she will be satisfied only by undertaking the story.

When she sits down to organize and write a complex piece, she is sensitive to each problem she faces. She can sense when her story elements provide an opportunity for creative handling and, just as important, when to stop trying to toy with a story and bang it out straight.

She's a fluent thinker. She knows when she needs ideas, and can call up a great number of relevant ones from her memory, giving herself more combinations to play with—more potential story angles to choose from.

She's flexible. She can look at a style of story structure that has solved dozens of tricky pieces for her in the past and realize that it won't get her out of this jam. She'll instead bend the old structure until it fits the new set of story components. If she stumbles on a completely new pathway—a story structure she has never seen anyone try before—she does not cringe; she has the audacity to assume that she may be the one who will make a new style work.

She's a better analyzer than her colleagues. She understands the amount of gritty effort she must put into studying her story components before the writing can begin. She understands that creative writing results from the new combination of old ideas, complex patterns formed from simple patterns, and the juxtaposition of elements that previously seemed unrelated. She has an unmatched talent for synthesizing, for redefining.

She concentrates on seeing through and beyond the obvious, the trivial. She prides herself on a deeper understanding of things. She considers herself able to penetrate further than her colleagues, to grab a topic and write the definitive version.

And sometimes it all comes together. And sometimes . . . nothing works. But the effort is always there, the search for an opening, the attempt by the reporter to liberate her creative potential when the time is right.

We saw in Chapter 7 that thinking in a right-brain frame of mind can unleash a writer's most intense artistic impulses. But to build a complete creativity filter, you need to give yourself more than a subjective edge. You must also study the way creativity is exhibited, and build a series of more objective tests that can be employed whenever you go looking for a creative solution.

To begin with, remember that our creative reporter is not as different as she seems. Her mind simply works harder at finding a pattern in the deluge of words, thoughts, events, and readers that fill her life. She envisions the potential combinations of these forces and picks the ones that best lead to story ideas and, subsequently, to story structure. She does all of this before she lays a finger on the keyboard. What makes writing such an intriguing act is the knowledge that she will never do it perfectly. There are too many variables, too many unknowns for her to pull all the forces into harmony. If she can walk away from a project having achieved 90 percent of what she dreamed of, she feels wildly successful.

Sometimes Ms. Turner's struggles sound like those of a woman on the verge of a psychopathic act, and if you're fond of Sigmund Freud, you may agree that there is little difference between the burden of a creative flow and an epileptic fit. Freud saw man unavoidably plagued by discontent as the result of conflict between his unconscious sexual and aggressive impulses and society's constraints. To reconcile the two pressures, he said, man seeks "defense mechanisms." If the mechanism is considered unacceptable by society—say, molesting children—the man is labeled maladaptive or psychopathological. But if the defense mechanism is one of sublimation—one in which he directs his energies into culturally approved behavior such as writing, painting, boxing, or political campaign organizing—society usually treats him well.

Creativity, Freud said, involves abandoning the world of reality for fantasy to provide an outlet for unsatisfied unconscious energies. Yet when you read any writer you admire, you can see that his injection of creativity is controlled. Had he indulged himself any more, had he not kept as much controlled balance between reality and fantasy, his approach to the story would not have worked. The closer you get to the edge, the more careful you need to be.

All great thought, all invention, rests on this balance, and yet the news business—like most other businesses—rarely takes it into account. News operations are structured on the same kind of flowchart, chain-of-command, area-of-responsibility mentality that most large enterprises use. When editors are trained (normally an unplanned, helter-skelter process), it is with an eye to structure. They are becoming managers. They have obligations to certain deadlines and processes. They have a loosely prescribed quota of stories that should be produced each day or week or month. They rarely are warned by their supervisors to give equal consideration to newsgathering proposals that don't quite fit into the paper's organizational structure.

The management of creativity ("the scheduling of invention," one researcher wryly calls it) has drawn considerable study since World War II. Courses on the management of research and development now flourish, but it seems impossible for them to reconcile the unpredictable, illogical thread of creativity with the fact that managers must constantly focus their efforts on controlling the activities of other people. The nature of creativity is that it breaks from established patterns and rules. How can a boss tolerate that and still run his system?

That question does not have to be answered in the newsroom; it merely needs more consideration by editors and reporters. Early in this book, we offered Rule Number 1 ("There are no rules") as something to keep in mind when pondering mental attitudes. Rule Number 1 is also a helpful guide inside the newsroom. If an idea is good, who cares how many rules it breaks? Give it a chance, test it, weigh it, but don't dismiss it outright. The rule causes a lot of grief, but it also produces greatness.

Editors and reporters have to look more closely at how well creative powers are being used. Many news reporters develop only a fraction of their talents because they work for editors whose ability to articulate judgment doesn't go beyond descriptions like "bright," or "cute," or the ever-present "reads well." Not working under a literate, refined system of criticism, the reporter faces a long, painful struggle to learn his own flaws and correct them by comparing his stories with those of better, more experienced reporters. Certainly, if he has the desire he can improve in that fashion, but why make it so hard on him? Why not give him some help?

A sensitive editor can save a reporter literally years of heartaches by offering a single sentence that sums up a dilemma the reporter may feel but can't interpret. Imagine a young reporter whose feature stories are excessively flamboyant (too sugary, too eager, the product of strained writing) being told by an editor, "I'd like you to do a better job of combining your uninhibited, impulsive ideas with rational control. I mean, you can be silly, but when you get that way, it's more important than ever that you concentrate on disciplined silliness."

Not enough editors like to talk about balancing extremes. Most of them would shoot the kid down. What they and their reporters should be concentrating on is *when* to go searching for a creative impulse and what to expect. As you read the following considerations, think about the stories you've had trouble writing, or stories you've read with disfavor.

Do the right conditions exist? Do you have enough related material in your memory to produce a clever or inspired angle for this story? If you've interviewed a Jewish immigrant from the Soviet Union, do you know anything about that immigration controversy to augment the interview? If not, the possibility of a creative approach is limited; you're forced to rely on the elements that surfaced during your conversation, or to supplement your memory with research.

How good a job can you do of sorting out the additional elements your memory feeds you? You may have triggered a heavy flow of peripheral ideas about immigration, or Russia, or Jews. Have you selected the proper ones to integrate into your story? Have you been influenced by the order in which they jumped into your head, or have you judged them on their merits?

Did some of the story elements suddenly leap out at you? That can be a good sign, because one test of the creative thought process is the vibrancy of the elements that are to be combined—they must stand out from their surroundings.

Do these impulses seem to be in a sufficiently free, unattached state? Make sure they are, because if the ideas you wish to combine are too rigidly tied to larger ideas, the new combination of thoughts you wish to construct may be artificial. You may wind up forcing an inappropriate or inaccurate structure. The right-brain style of outline is a valuable way of avoiding this hang-up because it allows you to view the relationships among your facts more clearly.

Finally, if the conditions do seem to exist for a unique, creative combination of ideas, make sure you have a feeling that the elements truly fit together, that they somehow merge like pieces of a jigsaw puzzle. If you can't feel that unity, you are probably kidding yourself.

Are you blocked? How often has this happened: The spark has hit, you've decided that the story warrants a creative approach, you have finally executed a masterful idea on your screen after extensive juggling—and now you're darned if you can figure out why it took you so long to go in the right direction. Why did you make so many wrong turns? Why didn't you reorganize the graphs sooner? Why did you have to spend two hours searching for the additional graph that brought the story into focus?

A variety of factors—most of them obvious, on second thought—can block creativity. Be on the lookout for potential blocks and you'll have a better chance of avoiding them. Again, a good procedure when you do become stuck is to ask yourself some questions.

Have you failed to correctly perceive and define the story elements? Have you fallen prey to wishful thinking and overrated the value of one or more elements? Were you overly ready to categorize your information? Did you judge it by its surface features, rather than by its significance? Did you forget the amount of energy that must be put into analyzing the story components and your goals for the story *before* you start to link various chunks of information into novel patterns? Experiments have found that the more creative scientific research worker devotes a proportionately larger part of his problem-solving activity to analysis; only after that analytical stage does he begin looking for a solution. Similarly, successful reporters often force themselves through an extra scan of their notes, resisting the temptation to rush to the keyboard and begin writing.

Do you really have as much information as you need? Do you have too much information, and are you intimidated by the excess? Have you made use of the proper information?

Has the syntax used by your sources cloaked your information in traditional terms and categories that prevent you from seeing the facts in a new, creative light?

Is there something in your personal makeup that is keeping you from seeing essential story elements and their relationships? Are you carrying a prejudice, a desire to tell the story for a particular gain? Are you hamstrung by a drive to show off your background knowledge? Try backing off a bit.

Try composing with a slightly smaller degree of expertise; try being a little dumber in order to be a little smarter.

Are you thinking the right way? You may be in the midst of *convergent* thought, in which a premium is placed on analysis and reasoning, but your story may defy that. The story elements alone may not lend themselves to a unique combination unless you bring something in from the outside. You may have to shift to *divergent* thinking, which emphasizes richness and novelty of ideas; it's a more playful way of solving a problem. Here's an example of a story that was written in standard, convergent style—and clearly could have benefited from divergent thinking:

> Despite President Clinton's warning last week that all Iraqis would be required to check with immigration officials before traveling overseas, international chess master Parach Shrizaz flew from Los Angeles to Munich Tuesday to visit his brother and inquire about European chess competition.
>
> The result: Immediately upon his return to New York, Shirazi was informed that he would be deported.
>
> "We thought everything would be OK," his young American bride of four months said tearfully. . . .

Look what could have happened if the reporter had been willing to shift gears and think in another direction. A small bit of divergent thought uncovers enough irony to grab the reader with far more force:

> In the game of chess, you can afford few mistakes.
>
> Parach Shrizaz, an international master at the game, made one too many.
>
> Despite President Clinton's warning last week that all Iraqis would be required to check in with . . .

Only if the reporter was willing to turn to a concept not directly related to the step-by-step chronology of the news story could that angle be found. All stories require both convergent and divergent thought, but each story is solved with a unique blend of the two. You must modify your approach from story to story.

Each of these blocks leads to the same essential question: Are you being stymied by forcing the wrong direction of attack? Are you being too rigid? Try to step away from the story. Remember, you need to balance a close involvement with the details of your story with a detached, imaginative view of the story's essence.

No matter how much you know about these blocks, sometimes that knowledge won't help. You'll suffer helplessly, waiting for inspiration, before giving up and cranking out an average piece. That's life. But don't be afraid to strain your mind the next time around. We have all been conditioned to fear our unconscious processes, to distrust them, to rely strictly on logical, rational forms of reasoning and writing. It takes courage to continue to give your intuitive side a chance. If you're lucky, it will lead to a heightened feeling that will make up for the routine nature of the majority of news work. Just the chance to test your creative powers to their limits once or twice a month is an opportunity most people would pay dearly for, if they only knew the emotional rewards.

For centuries, artists have spoken with awe of such experiences. Beethoven visualized and heard his instrumental music in its entirety while composing, and found there remained nothing for him to do but write it down. While composing *The Creation*, Haydn described a state of almost painful excitement: "My body would feel like ice, and then again, as if glowing in feverish heat." Others talk about words flowing spontaneously, against their will, so fast that the pen or typewriter could scarcely follow. The work became autonomous. The characters in a novel assumed an independent existence and took control, leading the writer where they wished to go. Sometimes these moments resembled a trance; other times the artist or writer was led along by a strange rhythm. Some were propelled by that fear that unless an idea was worked on immediately it would be lost.

And then, finally, the words would be on paper. A sensation of relief would begin to sweep over them and then, just as suddenly, they would have to check and double-check their work, afraid that they were wrong, afraid they had been carried away by a magical force too powerful to be confined by logic. "He to whom this emotion is a stranger," Albert Einstein said, "who can no longer wonder and stand rapt in awe, is as good as dead."

More on "Creativity" in the Appendix:

- Fourteen tips on how to make your writing more sophisticated

CHAPTER

9

Schizophrenia in Editing

The last word of the last rewrite has been typed. It's over. You give yourself an invisible pat on the back and breathe a well-deserved sigh of relief. For four days you pushed that story, and now the pressure's off, and you ease up.

You just made a big mistake. What you should be doing at this moment is pumping yourself up, becoming more vigilant, assuming a new perspective on the story, preparing to give yourself what doctors call a second opinion.

"That's the editor's job," you say. Wrong. It's your job. It's the final mental filter in our chain: the ability to harshly edit your story through another pair of eyes before it leaves your desk. It's the skill of looking at your masterpiece with a less romantic, much colder feeling—an attitude that challenges the choices you made during the composition phase; an attitude that doesn't presume that those choices were the right ones merely because they were hard.

This self-editing filter is another stage that too many reporters take for granted. Their failures cause many little, hidden problems and unnecessary grief, and also painfully illustrate the void that lies between the points at which a reporter's responsibility ends and an editor's begins.

The central fact is this: Most reporters in most news organizations do not have a great deal of confidence in the people who edit their copy. Reporters who work for a very large news operation may be lucky enough to have the guidance of an editor who specializes in the subject they're writing about, but usually the copy goes straight to the assignment desk, where it is read under pressure of time and volume, and then to the copy desk, where the editors usually concentrate on errors of commission, not omission.

Many copy editors are talented, but you should not rely on them. As we have stressed throughout this book, to develop your professional skills to the highest degree, you must become more self-reliant. You must seek out the hard choices. You must be willing to try to fill the little leadership gaps that plague all news operations.

What am I asking you to do? I am asking you to become selectively schizophrenic. I'm asking you to develop the ability to shift gears after you finish typing and before you start self-editing. At that moment, *become* an editor. Adopt the attitudes and perspectives that go with the job. Set your story aside for a minute, get up for a drink of water or walk around the office, and then return to your story with the eye of another person—somebody who has only peripheral familiarity with the subject of your story; somebody who will demand that the story snap out its essence, that its phrasing flow logically, that its purpose be clear. Don't read it on the computer screen; make a hard copy, a version that better resembles the way the story will feel when the reader holds it in his hands.

Those bursts of energy that came during the typing process may well have resulted in a variety of common oversights. We accept this, because the best reporters inject a power into their writing that overshadows appreciation of tiny detail. When you have a truly good story going, tiny detail is often not the first thing on your mind; you're grooving, the words are hitting, you're looking at the broad impact of your piece. Which is why surprisingly obvious mistakes can creep into an important story, even though the reporter has broken his back to collect and present the information. A crucial piece of background information may be missing; a key figure in the story may be named without sufficient explanation of his importance; the perspective paragraph (Chapter 5) may not be there. In all those cases, the reporter had dealt with the material so many times while preparing the story that he gradually began taking some elements for granted. He subconsciously began assuming that they were common knowledge.

In Chapter 4, we talked about knowing the reader as a safeguard against those kinds of mistakes. But because no one's perfect, we have to build in a second line of defense: your ability to aggressively edit your copy. Don't count on your editors to do this. How can they guarantee you that they'll always have the time—or the ability? Certainly you want them to review the story eventually, but for you there's a more important concern: to control your work to the greatest degree possible.

The average copy editor likes to avoid problems. When a passage in a story bothers him, he first tries to simplify it—deleting a troublesome sentence or phrase, for example. He is far less likely to amplify—to rewrite a paragraph, expanding it for precision. You're far better equipped to do that—if you can catch your own mistakes.

So wipe your mind clear. Take a deep breath. Concentrate. Use your imagination. Become someone else. It's nothing more than a game you play with yourself. Turning back to the typed story with a pencil in your hand, you've become Mr. Hyde, determined to put the work of the reporter, Dr. Jekyll, to the test.

Let's see what Jekyll has done. Here it is, a 2,000-word analysis of a one-year-old local rent control law. You, Hyde, don't know a lot about the background of the story you're holding, and that's all the better. Jekyll spent four long days on it, and who knows how much he wound up taking for granted? You, Hyde, will take nothing for granted.

First paragraph: Jekyll's story leads off with the fact that the area's landlords have had little luck in obtaining higher rents since the rent control law went into effect. But there's some important perspective missing here—the fact that the rent control law not only made rent increases hard to obtain, but also rolled back most rents to the previous year's level. Hyde finds this information when he gets to the sixth graph. Jekyll put it there because he was worried about its messing up the flow of his syntax; he talked himself into believing that the average reader knew of the rollback provision. Hyde is more objective. He weighs perspective against flow, decides that perspective is more urgent in a weighty analysis like this, and moves the rollback information up to the second graph.

Third paragraph: A small overstatement that Jekyll hoped would give a more substantial tone to the story has caused a problem. He is writing about "a strong majority of landlords" surveyed by a poll, when in fact that majority was 56.2 percent. "Strong"? Hardly. Hyde kills the adjective.

Fifth paragraph: Jekyll had this idea for a week and a half—a great image, he kept telling himself—and he was determined to use it. He wanted to describe the new power of the city's rent control board by saying, "The city's rent control establishment finds itself in the driver's seat. Local landlords, meanwhile, have their feet tied to the rear bumper of that driver's car, and are being dragged along cracked pavement."

Jekyll couldn't wait to put that in the story, but Hyde reads it with no such enthusiasm. In fact, Hyde realizes, there is more important factual material here. Jekyll has actually put together a good statistical analysis of a rent control system that had been described previously only by generalized rhetoric from landlords and tenants. With none of the ego problems that have hung up Jekyll, Hyde bumps the passage down into the eighteenth graph, and later in the day deletes it. Hardly a great image, Hyde notes ruefully.

As we've said, it's a game, but you have to play it. You have to invent ways to stay in control. If reporter-turned-Hyde doesn't get the story in shape, the werewolves of London on the copy desk—with a far less personal stake in the matter—will take over. And to the degree they sense the writer was not in control of the story, their willingness to make changes grows. Don't let them see any blood.

Some of this Jekyll-Hyde game playing is needed because deadlines make it impossible for you to let your story sit overnight and view it with a physically fresh eye the next day. But even when you have that luxury of time, concentrate on making this mental reporter-to-editor transition. Develop pride in your ability to subject your story to the most critical kind of dispassionate editing. Then think about parlaying that talent into better writing.

The relationship here, as with so many of the dynamics in news-thinking, is mathematical. To the extent you trust your editing ability, you can begin taking more risks as a writer. As Hyde's critical faculties are strengthened and sharpened, Jekyll's freedom to experiment is enhanced. For example, he can try beginning a story with four one-word paragraphs, no matter how dubious the technique seems, because he knows his editor alter ego will tear it up if it doesn't work.

Without Hyde, Jekyll might keep his creativity under wraps. Unless he was, say, 80 percent sure a style of writing or logic would be effective, he wouldn't attempt to use it. With a watchful Hyde, Jekyll can play with an idea at the typewriter even if he's only 10 percent sure it's a good one. Maybe by the time it is translated from his mind to the keyboard, it will work. Hyde will let him know.

Great reporters develop this confidence to take risks. There will always be times when Hyde's judgment will not suffice and you'll have to bounce an idea off a real editor; there will be other times when Hyde will simply be wrong, and your editors will tell you you've gone too far.

Schizophrenia in editing is this book's final filter, but it is probably the first thought strategy that will result in some immediate payoffs. By concentrating harder on editing your copy, you should quickly begin to catch flaws.

The majority of the other filters, especially ones such as creativity and sequencing, appeal to a long-term goal, a hope that a year from now you can look back at your work and see an improvement, an awareness. There should be more sensitivity, more perspective, more variety, more intelligence in your writing. We're hoping this will have come about because you were willing to think about your talents in higher, more challenging terms; because you were willing to engage in some deep professional and personal introspection. That change doesn't happen overnight, and nobody can help you achieve it; it comes from your soul if you want it badly enough. It's a long, hard climb. To make sure you get through it in one piece, read the next—and last—chapter.

More on "Schizophrenia in Editing" in the Appendix:

- One reporter's tips for ruthlessness in cutting fat
- Making sure each paragraph plays a specific role
- When leisureliness sabotages structure

10 Coping with Pressure

Stress is often used as a synonym for pressure, but technically it is the response of the body to any demand made upon it. (Scientists refer to the cause of stress as the *stressor.*) The late Dr. Hans Selye of Montreal, the leading stress researcher of his time, dramatically expanded interest in stress by pinpointing the body's response technique, a mobilization of defensive reactions involving the pituitary and adrenal glands. This same reaction occurs in response not only to physical injury, but also to a wide range of psychological condi—

WAIT! Who has time to talk about this? The phone on your desk in the newsroom is ringing! C'mon, pick it up. On the other end you hear an angry voice tearing into you for the story that appeared in this morning's paper.

Now, you broke your butt on that story and you're already a little peeved about not receiving as much praise as you expected. As the caller's attack continues, your brain launches a process as old as your cave-dwelling ancestors. It prepares you to fight back. You can feel your insides tense as you prepare your verbal comeback.

There will be a crucial difference between you and the caveman, however. As the caveman saw his attacker coming, his endocrine system began producing the arousal hormone adrenaline, which alerted and aroused the body by mobilizing sugar into the blood and redistributing it to the body's potential "action centers." Later, as the conflict began, his nervous system released a larger amount of the chemical noradrenaline, which helped maintain blood pressure.

But in your telephone clash, there is no violence; there is merely the *anticipation* of it. As a result, your body releases mostly adrenaline, not noradrenaline. You are aroused and ready—needlessly. The visceral part of your brain has detected a physical threat, and has placed your body's defense mechanisms on alert, even though there is no physical danger. And that can cause problems. Experts have found that the rush of chemicals in these repeated, unneeded stress reactions has disturbing physical effects. It can cause physical illness, such as ulcers and hypertension, and an unpredictable array of mental problems as well.

That rush is what you're getting on the phone. You put down the receiver, having argued back successfully, but still feeling a peculiar sensation that most of us write off as anger. Subtly, the damage has been done.

Pressure of even the most temporary variety can sap your mind's ability to process information, so you have to be on guard, regardless of how resilient you think you are. It is sadly inevitable: By our late twenties and thirties, our bodies begin to feel the strain. What were once little pressures begin to take a heavier toll. Parents die, marriages break up, children are born and raised. You can run but you can't hide. Life's pressures do increase, and it becomes harder to keep up with any job—particularly a news job—without bending.

You may be too worried about where to find a job to mull over the question of adjusting to one, but file the contents of this chapter in a corner of your mind just the same. It will come in handy. For now, let's get back to that angry caller in the newsroom and the angry response that began to well up inside you.

In any news operation, you're certain to find reporters and editors who, somehow, enjoy that sort of confrontation. They seem to seek it out. Sometimes they act like a drug addict looking for a fix, and in that light it is fascinating to consider a Canadian government study that said:

> Amphetamines . . . are in many ways similar to the body's own adrenaline. These drugs normally evoke an arousal or activating response not unlike one's normal reaction to emergency or stress.

Amphetamine addicts are called "speed freaks." They are often hostile, aggressive, and suspicious. The news world is full of hard-charging reporters with similar behavior—and similar cravings. They have found a cheaper source of drugs: their own bodies. Yet they, like the speed freak, will eventually pay.

Various studies disagree on the amount of damage occupational stress—your workload, your pressures, your tendency to strive—does to your health. To many people, a sense of challenge and achievement in the face of some pressure is necessary for satisfaction. Yet news work is clearly an area in which pressure can get out of hand, and safeguards are too often lacking.

The body's misuse of the stress response, as described earlier, is only one example of how man's control of his environment has drastically outpaced his evolutionary progress. Consider your eyes. A thousand years ago, man used his eyes largely for long-distance tasks, like hunting and fishing. Now we spend much of our time doing close-up work, such as reading from books and screens. The resulting stress—the pressure on the eyes to adapt—has created a culture of myopic people.

So it has gone with the adrenal gland's instinct for survival. The gland has yet to completely adjust to our rapidly acquired control of a once savage environment; it doesn't know the dinosaurs are extinct. It responds when it doesn't have to, and the result has been deadly to our culture of workaholics and strivers addicted to doing business at a compulsive, chaotic, aggressive, unhealthy pace.

Occupational stress studies have grown increasingly popular, but there is little evidence of a researcher's having investigated the news business and the effects of its pressure (not even in Selye's 1,256-page landmark study, *Stress in Health and Disease*). Businessmen, skydivers, frogmen, air traffic controllers—even coastal fishermen and Israeli kibbutz members—have been studied, but we in news are left with less-formal conclusions about the risks we take.

For example, there was the folksy little item the *Des Moines Register* printed a while back, which quoted a small-town editor who quoted a Farm Bureau member who quoted a psychologist as saying, "The fear of drowning, bankruptcy, or plunging into flames from an aircraft is less frightening than appearing like an idiot in print."

No matter how much you enjoy pressure at work, you are continually confronted with the necessity to exceed your tolerance. Gradually you adjust, and your tolerance level is raised a few more notches. Eventually you may reach a high, frightening cliff where you must choose between your health and your responsibility for doing your job the right way, as defined by yourself and your bosses.

No one can work in news without at least occasionally approaching that precipice. But you can control the frequency of such encounters by taking a hard look at your relationship to the job, by refusing to take for granted decades of prattle about the craft's unbearable pressure. You have to begin to do a better job of analyzing where your job pressures come from and how often you needlessly encourage them. As Hans Selye suggested to his audiences, "You cannot control your mother-in-law, but you can control the way you respond to her."

It's not the pressures of work that screw up your mind and body—it's your *response* to the pressures. Begin by surveying the job and your response to its demands. Categorize the stress that you can control. Then start looking at the other kinds of situations, those in which you don't feel able to control your response to pressure. Here you have to look at the source of the pressure and try to limit it without losing your effectiveness.

Don't feel guilty about admitting you're under too much pressure. In many offices, the credo is that you're not truly effective unless you're accomplishing your goals under strain, and for a while that works. You put a little more pressure on yourself, you push a little further, you absorb a little more tension, your work improves, and you get more done. But eventually you cross your line, an invisible barrier where pressure ceases to be beneficial and begins to erode your performance. Your body's reaction to pressure may first cause subtle changes in your physical stamina, making you increasingly vulnerable to mental errors as you work the same long hours. Where's the effectiveness in that?

The battle is to keep enjoyable, competitive hard work from being taken over by the insidious Protestant work ethic, a good idea that clearly got out of control. Four hundred years ago, French theologian John Calvin began insisting that every occupation—not merely the clergy—could be a "calling." You, the simplest of workmen, could assure yourself of a place with God by bringing to your work the qualities of thrift, honesty, abstinence, and industry.

Today, newsrooms are littered with burned-out 45-year-old reporters and editors, a bitter parody of the concept of work as religious pursuit. Thousands of men and women—victims of their own obsessive-compulsive behavior—have been sacrificed. Their jobs became cloaked in unhealthy and often counterproductive habits. The choice was between mere health and a career.

Because there hasn't been much of an effort in news work to fight that kind of momentum, you'll have to wage your own battle. If and when that vague feeling rears its head, suggesting that there is something wrong with the way you push yourself, take some time and look for a compromise—a balance, a level of physical and mental pressure that is good for you, a line you will try not to cross.

Gradually you will find that you—not the news circumstances, not your boss—are responsible for a certain percentage of line-crossings. In the intensity you exhibit at work, the amount of time you spend rethinking a story you wrote the other day, and the amount of anxiety you unleash worrying about career advancement, part of the pressure comes from a needless but persistent sense of obligation to be "serious," or to follow others' behavior. Don't fall for it.

Analyze your work environment and your perception of it, much as you scan the components of a story before you write. As in writing, there are important, sensitive choices to make. When is it helpful to push yourself, and when is it counterproductive? How have you built up unwarranted tension? How can you change your work routine without diminishing your effectiveness?

Unlike the process of newswriting, however, there is no editor here, no one to tell you whether you've made the right choice. You're on your own. Your decisions about how and whether to balance your pressure load won't be judged for years or decades, and even then only imprecisely by your body.

As hard as they try to find ways to preserve the sanity of the "driven" businessman, psychological counselors keep coming back to the factor of motivation. If the executive believes that his compulsive behavior is vital to the organization, if he feels that a painful level of pressure is a price that has to be paid for success or respect, he cannot be pulled away from it. But when his perception improves—when he realizes that many of his obsessive habits are *counterproductive* to his performance—he can force himself to change. He can work even harder without paying a physical price.

Awareness builds the ability to control some of our response to pressure. That realization, in turn, builds confidence in our ability to reduce other stress factors, always with the goal of sacrificing only unneeded pressure, retaining the level of tension that works for us, pushes us in the right direction.

When job pressure plagues you, try making a rough mental list of the pressure points, the factors that seem the most stressful. A sample might include, in no order of importance:

Unpredictable overtime

Deadlines

Night work

Frequent fear of being unable to obtain vital information

Frequent letdowns when anticipated information does not surface

Fear of looking foolish in print

Distrust of editors, anxiety over lack of control once copy is in their hands

Anger provoked by criticism

Prejudice, suspicion, and hostility from uncooperative sources or readers

Lack of leadership or direction from editors

Inability to meet or understand editor's expectations

Continual demands to face the unknown

Constant awareness of what work is due tomorrow

Pressure for productivity at the expense of quality

Boredom from insufficient assignments, lack of challenge

Need to play office politics in order to advance

How often does each situation surface? Is it more likely to be caused by circumstances of the news flow or by individuals? How often are you the individual responsible for heightening the pressure? How often does your performance improve as a result of your willingness to put more pressure on yourself? How often does your performance falter? When you put more pressure on yourself, how often is it done with a precise goal in mind? How often is it done out of a general, obligatory feeling that you should be working harder? Which of those two attitudes produces the best results?

In short, separate the pressures that are uncontrollable or beneficial from the ones that are controllable or unhelpful. After you've made that distinction, there are tougher decisions to be made. Of the uncontrollable/ beneficial group—the inevitable pressures—which, if any, are taking too great a toll on your emotions or your body? Is there room to change the way you work? Is a more drastic change needed?

Advocates of holistic health, who claim that physical and mental well-being are completely dependent on each other, are trying to persuade people to take a closer look at the connection between their work and their bodies, between their professional and emotional sides. They might tell you, for example, that introverts tend to make better use of information stored in their memory (in-depth reporting) than do extroverts, and that introverts make the best use of their powers if not driven hard (vulnerability to deadlines). Extroverts, on the other hand, tend to enjoy noise and bright colors, seem to actively seek stimulation, and tend to remain stable under pressure.

The implications of such studies are obvious for an editor making story or beat assignments. For reporters, the evidence again underlines our theme: Are you working in the right kind of job? If the pressure load seems unbearable, is it possible you are having to fight too hard against your personality?

The effects of pressure usually show up first as fatigue, and it is here that our system of newsthinking filters can temporarily stave off the damage. Normally, fatigue saps your information-processing system in devious, often unfelt ways. There is little remedial action that can be taken when your long-term memory fails to supply a key connection with new information, when your short-term memory isn't able to hold as many chunks of information as usual, when your system of sequencing doesn't provide as many alternative combinations as usual, or when the story slides into print without a perspective paragraph. You're too tired to be aware of those voids.

At least, the average reporter is. Working by a casually constructed system, he isn't remotely aware of the order in which he usually processes a story, and so he doesn't know which steps are most susceptible to fatigue and which are the most important to preserve. He responds to pressure crudely—holding up as long as possible, but eventually caving in, accepting the inevitable slack-off in performance.

But with a conscious system of filters, you have a better chance of sacrificing as little as possible to unanticipated pressure and fatigue. When you feel things closing in around you, when you realize your mind is not working at normal capacity, start concentrating on the filters we've discussed in previous chapters. Make sure your story has been tested against each one. That checklist at least assures you that you've maintained your basic thought process. Every skilled professional—doctor, pilot, athlete, you name it—has this kind of safety valve, a strategy to rely on when he or she gets into trouble.

As your sophistication allows you to combine several thinking or writing maneuvers into one step, you'll be able to operate with fewer conscious decisions than most reporters. Because your knowledge of story structure gives you a superior awareness of patterns, you'll have an edge in anticipating the kinds of decisions you'll have to make. Because you have polished your thought process, you'll need less effort to correct your errors. Because you understand the unity of listening, thinking, and writing, you'll be better at pacing your work so that it remains within your capacity. You'll anticipate your weak spots; you'll head them off at the impasse. This collective confidence will make you less anxious than the average reporter who shows up at work with a bad head cold, hoping to coast through the day, only to be confronted with an assignment to cover a detailed embezzlement trial.

Again, the solution is mathematical. When circumstances force you to cross your line of balance—to undergo more pressure than your maximum—measure how far across the line you've had to go, and then increase your vigilance by the same amount. You can do this only if you have developed an understanding of your talents and limitations.

Suppose, after all this, you still can't keep things under control? Suppose you find yourself crossing your line of demarcation more frequently than you'd like? Suppose some deep need—the desire for constant success and approval, or for immediate gratification—just can't be met? Then you have to ask yourself The Big Question: "Is it worth it?" For too long, we have begun such introspection by asking an unrealistic question: "Am I cut out for news work?" Look: *Nobody* is cut out for news work as it is currently practiced. It violates too many concepts of civilization. It asks you to throw out too much of your passion for life. It pressures you to trade spontaneity for logic. It commands you to quantify a world that resists cut-and-dried descriptions. And yet, somehow, it has a magic about it, addictive enough to pull you along. When you are no longer sure it is worth it, ask yourself the real questions: "Are the sacrifices I have to make in my personality in order to work in news worth the effort? Am I willing to operate without ever reaching a consistent emotional balance? If that balance is my highest aspiration, where do further sacrifices have to be made—in my work, or in my personality?"

At conferences throughout the world, Hans Selye was constantly asked for his advice on how to cope with stress, and he persistently insisted there is no miracle. "The final solution is a psychological one," he'd say. "You must get people to adopt a code of behavior, a code that transcends politics." This code encourages the optimum blend of stimulation, arousal, and conflict. It ties your feelings and your goals together, creating a level of tension that your body and mind will instinctively seek, much as you seek the proper volume when you turn on your CD player. Some people like it louder than others.

No one defines that level for you; the best they do is leave you to wallow in generalities like "tight-assed" or "mellow"—sluggish words, each with enough unpleasant connotations to drive any intelligent person away. In our business, there is precious little time or encouragement for you to pursue the search for the right level of pressure to govern your life. Yet unless you can construct such a state of grace, you will not fulfill your potential as a writer.

More on "Coping with Pressure" in the Appendix:

- Ten things reporters want from their editors
- Ten things editors want from their reporters

APPENDIX

A collection of excerpts from the *Los Angeles Times* newsletter on writing, "Nuts & Bolts" from 1998–2000, arranged to focus on themes from the chapters of *Newsthinking*.

Chapter 1: Your Stance

The Genesis of Good Ideas

What we write about is often more important than the techniques we use to make the story pretty. Newspapers continue to suffer from too many stories that feel obligatory or flat or formatted and too few that brim with a sense of discovery—a natural enthusiasm that comes from looking at the world in a fresh way. It isn't merely language that hooks the reader and carries him along, it's the ideas—your ability to make him think about something in a way he never thought about it before.

Here are four essays from Times *reporters that provide insight into attitudinal technique—the intellectual stances that can make you more sensitive to good ideas.*

Imagine the Broadest Context Possible

Many of us have written the story of a parent fighting for social change after losing a child to homicide or disease. And many of us slapped ourselves in the head when we read Mark Fritz's piece about how common this syndrome has become, and how it can lead to poorly thought-out social policy. It was so obvious! So how come the rest of us didn't think of it? (Confession: I once wrote about a Riverside, Calif., father's successful crusade to ban lawn darts after one of them accidentally struck and killed his daughter, and until I read Mark's article it never dawned on me that what I'd chronicled was part of something grander.)

Ask Mark how he connected the dots, and he responds:

I live in the wilds of western New Jersey, where the biggest fear isn't crime, cow pies, or drive-bys, but a tick the size of a decimal point that might be carrying Lyme Disease, a rarely fatal but potentially debilitating yet easily treatable illness caused by a spiral-shaped bacteria borne by a bug that can burrow into your eyebrow and suck your blood for two days before it drops, now looking like a fat asterisk, onto the copy of "Nuts & Bolts" you happen to be reading. Last year, under pressure from Northeast politicians, the FDA rushed the approval of a vaccine that seemed to work for some people. Sometimes.

I like stories about things that change collective human behavior, so I thought this news peg might warrant a quick trip to the Connecticut city where the affliction was discovered to see how Lyme the disease had changed Lyme the town, a woodsy epitome of upscale exurbia.

The most interesting thing I found was the Lyme Disease Foundation, a nonprofit group founded by a couple whose child had died of mysterious ailments that the family had become convinced were caused by a Lyme-carrying tick that must have bit the mom while she was pregnant, though the link was never proven. Their belief that Lyme disease was much worse and more prevalent than the evidence indicated was taken at face value by so many newspapers, that a couple of scientists tried to point out that these folks were letting their personal agenda distort the empirical facts. Cooler heads claimed the foundation was panicking people into thinking they had the disease when they didn't, and had opened the door to countless Lyme-curing quacks.

I tucked this example of obsessive parental advocacy away for a bit, looking for parallels elsewhere. If something is happening somewhere, something similar is usually happening somewhere else for somewhat the same reason, which sometimes means, voila, a trend (which sometimes unravel so slowly they aren't noticed for decades).

Some months later, President Clinton signed a new law called the "Jeanne Cleary Act" that compelled colleges to compile new sets of campus crime statistics for the Department of Education. This law required them to begin collecting and collating crimes that occurred in places adjacent to campus or were merely frequented by students. Having dropped out of one school nestled in the peaceful countryside of western Michigan, and attended another that mingled colorfully with the crack alleys and hooker promenades of midtown Detroit, I wondered about how this one-size-fits-all law would work. I noticed an item in a higher education trade journal about the legislation, and it quoted some school officials as saying the new law, which toughened an already confusing older law, was so contradictory and difficult to decipher that schools needed to pull cops off the streets to manage compliance.

It turned out that Jeanne Cleary, a freshman from a well-to-do family, was the victim of a torturous campus rape and murder that had compelled her parents to go on a mission to change the way schools catalogued and chronicled crimes on campus. They had succeeded in getting two sweeping federal laws and 13 state statutes enacted in little more than a decade. Lobbyists, lawmakers, and even tough-on-crime prosecutors admitted they often were too intimidated to point out the flaws of these laws when confronted with the mind-bending manifestation of every parent's worst nightmare.

Their comments, campaigns, convictions and even their web site were so strikingly similar to the Lyme folks' that it took only minutes to find other analogies in crime, product liability, and disease policy. I passed a note on to my editor, Bret Israel, who talked with colleagues Scott Kraft and Tom Furlong, and more analogies poured forth: MADD, Megan's law, missing kids on milk cartons, Three Strikes prison sentencing, the Superfund's origins as an outgrowth of a mother's complaint about the Love Canal. Parents whose kids suffered brain damage because of an infinitesimally possible yet unproven link to the whooping cough vaccine had morphed into a movement opposed to childhood vaccines—the lack of which probably kills more kids in the world than anything else. All relied on media stories that—whether the killer was a paroled child molester or a disposable cigarette lighter—sounded eerily similar, and sometimes tritely formulaic.

This wasn't an easy story to write. Many parents had accomplished incalculable good after suffering incomprehensible loss. Yet their missions were so uniform in the arc they followed that it cried out to be covered as a collective phenomenon that increasingly produced what some rarely covered critics said was bad law.

A psychologist specializing in parental grief told me that embarking on a mission, in fact, is a common reaction to the loss of a child. But there were other things at play that became apparent by imagining the broadest context possible and talking to people from other, seemingly unrelated fields: The growth of the Internet and its ability to instantly link like-minded people; this decade's unparalleled demand for tough anti-crime laws; the increasingly imitated success that AIDS and breast cancer advocates have had on influencing the priorities of federal disease policy; the two political parties' war to one-up each other on people-pleasing legislation; and this generation's rise in consumer protection and product liability lawsuits—all have combined to give enormous public policy power to pitiable parents just trying to cope.

Sure, far too many news stories are twisted into symbols of the Zeitgeist, but today's Zeitgeist (I know, you German speakers, it's a redundant term) compared to yesterday's is a terrific source for stories and a good way to broaden the context enough to find angles that challenge the surface assumptions that lead to formulaic approaches. I firmly believe that every story we cover is a tiny part of a larger one that sometimes eludes our grasp. Too often, we forget that what we mostly cover are aberrations from the norm, and we have a tendency to treat a statistical cluster of aberrations themselves as trends while missing the larger picture, which is sometimes as interesting as the aberration itself.

Excerpt:
. . . The Clearys remain undeterred. Theirs is a classic American story of contemporary activism, a wounded family's odyssey endlessly replayed, from Megan's Law to missing children on milk cartons. Thanks to the unlimited power of parental grief to attract media and sway lawmakers, lawn darts in toy stores and drawstrings on children's clothing are banned. A vaccine comes to market earlier than originally intended. A child's sickness is linked to Love Canal, spawning the Superfund.

And at the center of them all so often stands a tragic tale, a family calamity transformed into arresting allegory, a freak occurrence offered up as a terrifying trend.

Parental grief, in fact, has become one of the most powerful political forces in the country. Already, the massacre at a high school in Littleton, Colo., has inspired a parents' group modeled after Mothers Against Drunk Driving that aims to toughen gun laws and, if history is any guide, will inevitably broaden its agenda.

"You see this on hundreds of different things," says Burdett Loomis, a University of Kansas expert on interest groups. "What is fascinating to me is that a lot of times the power is in the story itself, the narrative. The power it has over legislatures. Anecdotes become the evidence."

Though it can be politically dangerous to oppose teary-eyed parents from middle-class America clutching photos of children killed by what they are certain is some institutional defect, there are signs of an emerging backlash.

Chief Justice William H. Rehnquist recently ripped Congress for churning out laws "to appear responsive to every highly publicized societal ill or sensational crime."

In February, an American Bar Assn. task force said 40% of the federal criminal laws passed since the Civil War had come in just the last three decades—often "in patchwork response to newsworthy events" rather than "an identifiable federal need."

The bar says the last Congress alone slogged through 1,000 new crime proposals, with some of the voguish laws passed in recent years—including those against drive-by shootings, interstate spouse abuse and murder committed by escaped convicts—so superfluous they were never used.

Even MADD founder Candy Lightner says the politics of grief have seized control of the political system. "How are you going to say 'no' to a crying mother?" she says. "The legislature winds up acting emotionally, and you have all these ridiculous laws passed that don't do a hill of beans. I can relate to it, because I used to do it too."

Look for the Nexus Where Several Fields Intersect

Our paper's emphasis on geographical and topical beats, as well as on increased formatting, conspires against the kind of eclectic thinking in which a reporter finds a story in that rich soil where two or more seemingly unrelated fields intersect. One of the best at doing this is business writer Sharon Bernstein, who describes how she got jazzed by news that Eli Lilly & Co., the pharmaceutical company that makes Prozac, was about to air a 30-minute television infomercial promoting the antidepressant.

When I first heard the news, the old-line business reporter in me wasn't all that impressed. But the former media writer in me was floored.

They're going to do *what?* And they're going to run these things *when?* In the middle of the night so depressed people can see them?

I knew this was a hell of a story. But it wasn't obvious to a lot of people until it was all done. The *New York Times* and *Wall Street Journal* had passed the information on to their marketing writers, who devoted all of one paragraph to the topic in columns on new advertising campaigns. Although my editor, Annette Haddad, immediately saw the value of the story, some people on our business desk didn't think it was that important.

But from my perspective—having covered entertainment, business, and health care, and having often thought about how marketing and media affect people—the story was a natural. To pull it off, though, I had to rely on skills honed in very different fields.

To gather the elements necessary for a good financial story, I relied on techniques learned by covering business during two stints in my career: I found out why the company felt it needed to market Prozac, what the goals of the campaign were, and what it cost. But to cover the program properly as media, I also relied on skills from my days of covering TV and entertainment.

I watched the show and took notes. I interviewed the producer to find out what she had been trying to accomplish. In the story, I made sure to describe the program itself, quoting from the narration and describing the mood and the program's progress.

Putting those two fields together, I was then able to make the most important leap—understanding the program's importance as it related to health care. I found sources who were experts in health care and mass communications, and talked to them about the program, its positioning in the market and the financial goals of Eli Lilly in making the show.

The resulting story ran on A-1 and was picked up by many other media outlets. At a symposium on the health care business a few weeks later, it was quoted by the keynote speaker.

The Prozac story brought home to me something I had been trying to articulate for years: that the best stories come not from narrow specialization, but from the nexus of several fields. In my case, this happened entirely by accident. I bounced around to so many beats that I wound up, for example, covering business (the first time around) like a political reporter; then, when I switched to media writing, I covered entertainment with the understanding of a business reporter. And so on when I went back to metro news and then came back to business.

The resulting stories are kind of weird—maybe because they're written from something of an outsider's perspective—but they're full-bodied in a way that I think is important. They're more fun to write, too.

In a way, writing from several points of view is like learning several foreign languages. You reach for Italian and it comes out French. But the resulting patois can be the basis of a whole new language.

Excerpt (beginning with lead):

Borrowing a technique used to sell everything from exercise equipment to food dehydrators, the makers of the antidepressant Prozac have produced a 30-minute television infomercial to directly market to consumers the prescription-only drug.

The commercial, which is aimed mostly at women, will air in the middle of the night and on weekends, when company marketers believe more depressed people will be watching.

By producing the ads, Prozac manufacturer Eli Lilly & Co. is aggressively stepping up to the plate in a controversial new area of marketing that many pharmaceutical companies see as their best hope for new sales in the era of managed care.

More and more, since rules on advertising drugs on television were eased in late 1997, drug makers are turning to consumers, rather than doctors and hospitals, to create demand for their products.

The question of marketing a psychiatric drug directly to consumers, however, goes to the heart of the controversy over whether pharmaceuticals should be advertised on television. Prozac, unlike drugs for allergies and hair loss, can have psychological side effects and is aimed at a condition that is often not easily treated.

"It's a trap," said George Gerbner, a telecommunications professor at Temple University in Philadelphia and author of the book *Alcohol, Tobacco and Other Drugs in the Mass Media.* "They're trying to appeal to and exploit the most vulnerable people."

The Prozac commercial, which appears to be the first half-hour advertisement for a psychiatric drug, is part of Lilly's bold campaign to shore up the $2.8-billion drug's lead among antidepressants.

. . . "You've got to have mixed feelings on this," said Lawrence Wallack, who specializes in mass media and public health issues at UC Berkeley and Portland State University in Oregon. "Depression is a big issue, and the more public discussion of it the better. But you can't get around the fact that it's an infomercial. It's a sales pitch."

Introduced in the United States in 1988, Prozac was the first of a new breed of antidepressant medications called selective serotonin reuptake inhibitors. . . .

"Weigh Reality against Society's Expectations."
Greg Braxton's front-page piece in May, 1999, about the virtual whiteness of the coming network television season stood out as a strong moral statement by the

newspaper. Rather than writing about a questionable societal trend after interest groups or lawyers intervened, Greg's piece was a simple but important statement of a fundamental shift in programming: The networks, which had been creeping toward diversity, seemed to have retrenched in unison. (The usually hip Entertainment Weekly *didn't pick this up until July 30, using as an angle the NAACP's plans to protest, which came in a reaction to Greg's piece.)*

The story was—like Mark Fritz's parent-protest story—obvious in retrospect, and so is the lesson it teaches: Keep measuring reality against society's expectations. The story also reinforces Sharon Bernstein's point about finding stories where two fields collide—in this case, entertainment and race.

Greg explains:

Since coming on the TV beat in 1994, I have spent much of my time exploring minority images on dramas and comedies, and how race relations are handled on different shows. Pursuing this angle has resulted in a steady stream of stories—how comedies are more segregated than dramas, the unhappiness with black and Latino images, and how some popular series have been popular with white viewers but not minority viewers, and vice versa.

Just before the new fall schedules were announced, I got a sense that there would probably be little ethnic diversity in the new shows. But it didn't start to dawn on me, my colleague Brian Lowry, or my editor Betsy Sharkey that there would be virtually no minorities in a leading role, very few blacks in supporting roles, and virtually no Latinos or Asian Americans that were visible.

In New York in May, all of the television networks unveil their new programming before advertisers, showing them clips of all the new shows. I attended closed-circuit broadcasts of those presentations here. By the second day of watching pilots, it was obvious that there was a certain sameness to the looks of the shows. That was a sharp contrast to our anticipation of more integration, especially since there had been diversity in some of the hit shows, like *The Practice.* We assumed the pendulum was going to keep swinging in a direction of inclusion. I remember sitting in an ABC board room and being so shocked that the casts of the new shows—even ensemble casts of the new dramas—seemed to be all white.

Heightening the contrast further was the fact that I had heard several network executives say in previous years that diversity was very important to them. But from the clips and cast photos, it was clear that wasn't the case this time. Something had gone wrong. It was never anticipated that all of the major networks—Fox, CBS, NBC, and ABC—would all look the same.

I contacted the network executives and confronted them about the trend and their past promises. For the most part, they were responsive in explaining their rationale, and how they were *still* trying. When the story wound up on the front page, many of them clammed up.

It was only the beginning of what would turn out to be an ongoing series of stories examining diversity in television, which has turned out to be the hot-button issue clouding the new season.

Excerpt (beginning with lead):
The new prime-time television season has been unveiled, and guess who's not coming to dinner this fall.

Of the 26 new comedies and dramas premiering on the major broadcast networks—CBS, NBC, ABC, and Fox—not one features a minority in a leading role. Even secondary minority characters on these sitcoms and dramas are sparse, turning the TV lineup into a nearly all-white landscape.

There are few blacks in supporting roles on the shows, and Latinos, Asian Americans, Native Americans, and other ethnic groups are virtually invisible. And even Fox, a network that grew to prominence on the strength of shows targeted for and featuring blacks, may have only one regular black character on its entire schedule this fall.

The lack of minority characters has sent a shudder through an industry that has prided itself on being politically enlightened and progressive. Further, it is in direct contravention of network executives' repeated pledges to increase diversity in their shows.

Tom Nunan, entertainment president of sixth-ranked UPN, whose edgier programming strategy includes several shows featuring minorities in leading and supporting roles, said the lack of diversity on the major networks has been obvious for some time but is particularly evident in the new crop of prime-time series.

"It was really glaring at the upfronts," said Nunan, referring to the networks' announcement of the fall prime-time series lineup to advertisers last week in New York. Advertisers, in turn, will now decide how and where to spend roughly $6.5 billion to buy advertising time in advance of the season, which begins in mid-September. "It was a shortsighted approach that they took. When you realize how valuable the African American audience can be, and also any minority audience, [inclusion] shows respect to all Americans, not just one demographic group."

Among several high-profile shows with all-white casts are ABC's *Wasteland*, about six "twentysomethings" living in New York City and dealing with life after college; NBC's *Freaks and Geeks*, which features a group of teens attending a suburban high school in 1980; CBS's *Love or Money*, a comedy about romance in an upscale New York City apartment building; Fox's *Manchester Prep*, set at a prestigious New York prep school; and NBC's *Cold*

Feet, about three couples in various and differing stages of relationships.

Keep an Open Mind

Evelyn Larrubia heard about what sounded like a slam-dunk story: Some toy manufacturer was producing a set of figurines called "Homies" which clearly resembled Latino gang members. An outrage story, clear and simple. But by being willing to let the story take on additional complexities—rolling with the punches and keeping an open mind to a changing set of facts—Evelyn produced a far richer tale about two ways of looking at the world.

"Cultural toys." That's what the guy on the other end of the phone was calling them. Sure, some people have complained that they look like gang members, he conceded, but they're just ignorant.

This was not quite what I'd expected to hear when I finally tracked down David Gonzales, creator of those 1 3/4-inch Homies figurines that had cops and prosecutors up in arms.

I had gone out and bought myself a purseful of Homies figurines and stickers as soon as I heard about them. I saw the knit caps, the bulging muscles, the baggy pants and white tee-shirts, the bandana hanging out of one guy's back pocket, the teardrop that looked like a prison tattoo—I was sure this was going to be an easy, quick story. I mean, who wouldn't condemn toys dressed like gang members?

All I had to do was track down the company that made the toys, call a few Hispanic activists, add police and prosecutor quotes, and file it.

But now I had Gonzales talking, with a straight face, about low-rider Chicano kids as a *cultural phenomenon*. He told me his art was inspired by neighborhood people from the barrio. They weren't supposed to be bad, just authentic, he said. He was intelligent, well-spoken and sounded like a decent human being.

I didn't know if anyone would agree that these tiny, cartoonish Chicano toys were art, but it was worth a shot. Which meant my original idea of just calling people up and describing the little guys was not going to work. I mean, baggy clothes and bandanas? Nobody was going to defend that description on its face.

Nope, I had to take the Homies on the road. I showed them to kids, parents, community leaders. Those I couldn't get to personally I asked to look at pictures of the little guys on the manufacturer's web page.

Even then, plenty of people still hated them. They thought the toys were demeaning and demoralizing. They said Homies glamorized gang life and perpetuated negative stereotypes about Hispanics. But I didn't have to go very far to find others who actually saw these little Homies as a genre of art. At the very least, they said the toys and stickers were an honest portrayal of some people who lived in Chicano neighborhoods.

Excerpt:
. . . The Homies draw mixed reactions from Los Angeles area Latino community leaders, raising issues of dignity, stereotyping, and the right to artistic expression.

Some in the community agree that many of the images are nothing more than silly, harmless, or nostalgic portrayals of characters that have existed for decades.

"It's a form of art and I respect it as such," said Xavier Flores, head of both the local area Mexican American Political Assn. (MAPA) and the San Fernando-based social service agency Pueblo y Salud.

He said he has seen similar caricatures over the years and considers them a legitimate portrayal of disaffected Mexican American youth who feel neglected and rejected by the dominant culture. "It's art imitating life."

But other activists said they found the toys to be offensive.

"They are negative images. They perpetuate stereotypes," said Helen Hernandez, president and founder of the Imagen Foundation, which honors groups that portray Latinos in a positive light in film, television, and advertising. "Who is he kidding?"

"I believe in creative freedom, but I also believe in social responsibility," Hernandez said, disgust washing over her face as she examined the toys.

"They're cool! They're gangsters," said 9-year-old Gino Johnson, a sweet-faced third-grader at Vaughn Next Century Learning Center, who was interviewed at the Pacoima Boys and Girls Club on Thursday night. "Can I have this one?"

Details

Well-crafted disaster stories remind us how exhaustive reporting provides more real drama than dramatic language. The density of detail allows the writer to create one terse sentence after another, coming like waves, pounding the reality of the disaster into your soul with specific images.
Like this:

CAROLINA BEACH, N.C.—Hurricane Bertha smacked the Carolina coast Friday like the back of the devil's hand, hurling its 35-mile eye across Cape Fear, blinding the beachfront with rain, and wrecking homes and businesses with 105-mph winds that flung shards of glass through the streets.

Pay particular attention to what happens in the second paragraph:

> Skies darkened. Trees tumbled onto power lines and plunged thousands of people into a blackout. Riptides and 9-foot breakers crashed into boardwalks. A pleasure boat struck a major bridge and shut it down. One woman died in storm-whipped traffic, and six other people were hurt at Camp LeJeune, a Marine base near the North Carolina shore.

You've been reading the work of National's Richard E. Meyer, whose work speaks to a near-religious appreciation of detail. Rick explains:

Details are what put readers right there, where it happened, when it happened, in the shoes of the people I'm writing about. (Relevant details, of course. Irrelevant ones don't belong.)

When I'm doing rewrite on disasters, I like to pack the second and sometimes the third paragraph with the details that give this kind of immediacy. But it works just as well, sometimes even better, with feature pieces.

I try to remember the senses. A lot of what we know comes to us through our senses. Just watch *Sesame Street*. We learn four by *seeing* four apples, *hearing* four bells, *feeling* four fuzzy peaches.

So when I interview, I go through a litany of the senses.

Here are some questions from an old interview and the results in a feature story I wrote.

Q: Tell me about when you were a little girl and your grandmother came to visit. Picture her in your mind. What do you *see?*

From the story:

> Nana would arrive wearing a housedress and black shoes with laces and little heels. She carried a black vinyl purse with gold-colored clasps and black straps. Her hair was white. She tied it in two braids, which she pinned on top of her head.

Q: When Nana chewed out your father for whipping you, what did you *hear?*

From the story:

> She would haul herself up, double her fist, and yell: "If you ever hit anybody again with that belt, I'll take it and put it around

your neck." . . . Joe Horwat would squirm, back away, and flee into the garage. Julia could hear him throwing tools and spitting into the kerosene can where he washed car parts. She would chuckle.

Q: Julia, when your father came to visit you in the hospital, what did you *smell?*
From the story:

> She could smell the grease and his Lucky Strikes. She thought about the garage at home, and she wanted so much for him to pick her up and take her with him.

Q: When he leaned down and kissed your forehead, what did you *feel?*
From the story:

> She felt strength in his kiss. It was firm, even rough: a man's kiss.

Q: When the nurse came in to clean your teeth, what did you *taste?*
From the story:

> She could taste a cotton swab, along with two fingers.

Details. Get them all. Not just black shoes. Black shoes with laces and little heels. Not just cigarettes. Lucky Strikes. Details. Details. Individually, they are very important. But taken all together, they are more important still. They help you convey your subject to your readers not just at the level of what can be seen and heard and smelled and tasted, but taken all together they help you convey your subject at the level that Henry James called the "felt life."

Which is to say, they give your readers feeling for your subject that they just can't get otherwise.

Showing versus Telling

One of the most important questions a reporter can ask is: "Can I watch? Can I observe you in action? Can I see for myself?" So often this is the difference between ordinary and good stories. It's particularly true of human-interest stories and almost unfailingly true of profiles. A recent example was Patrick Goldstein's Sunday Calendar piece in the L.A. Times about a talented, abrasive TV producer named Aaron Sorkin. It was authoritative and honest, and continually paired Patrick's observations with revealing anecdotes. These two paragraphs are an example:

TV is not a medium for manic perfectionists. But as a former playwright, Sorkin values the word—and the sound of a word—so if he thinks a line of dialogue sounds off, he will unapologetically hit the brakes and stop the train to fix a loose coupling.

Raised in Scarsdale, N.Y., Sorkin always had a glib knack for dialogue. He prepared for his bar mitzvah by passing over the usual Torah study. "I went to Rabbi Greenberg and told him, 'I have a very good ear. Just speak [the Hebrew] into a tape recorder and I'll learn it. ' It's my gift. I can give the impression of being a very bright, interesting person that you'd want to invite over for dinner."

What set the piece apart was Patrick's ability to watch Sorkin in action. He describes his journey here:

The biggest challenge a writer faces covering the entertainment business today is obtaining access. The whole machinery of modern-day publicity is geared toward denying access—ensuring that reporters only get carefully controlled, bite-sized exposure to interview subjects, usually at quickie, sit-down meetings in hotel rooms held just before the premiere of a movie or TV show. It encourages a lot of make-nice stories that are great promotion for a movie, but it doesn't make for especially memorable journalism. When I was a kid, I remember being enthralled by magazine pieces like Gay Talese's "Frank Sinatra Has a Cold." It was a model of good showbiz journalism because Talese had total access—and knew what to do with it. You saw Sinatra, up close and personal, unrehearsed, with the kind of telling detail and intimate atmosphere that lets readers feel that they're on the inside too.

When I approached Sorkin about doing a piece on him, I already knew I had a good subject—a gifted writer in the midst of the high-wire act of writing two TV shows, *Sports Night* and *The West Wing,* at the same time. But I didn't just want to interview him about how he did it. I wanted to hear Sorkin blearily schmoozing with actors at 1:30 A.M. or see him, hopelessly behind schedule, giving a nervous director a souvenir *West Wing* cap instead of a finished script.

When I called Sorkin, I told him I wanted to see a little bit of everything that goes into making a TV show: table reads, rehearsals, story meetings, run-throughs, as well as the actual filming of an episode of each show. To his credit, he was generous with his time. And my editors, to their credit, gave me the time to go back for a third and fourth day, which paid off: Much of the best material in the story, especially Sorkin's frank description of his downward spiral into drug addiction, came from the final day of my visits.

As a reporter, the first day you visit a movie or TV set you're treated like an alien from another planet—everyone feels the presence of an outsider. The second day you're a little less intrusive. By the fourth day, if you haven't knocked over a key light or tried to pick up the star's girlfriend, people forget you're there. They stop being on their best behavior and worrying about what they're going to say around you—which is when you start to see a little whiff of reality. You also learn things that surprise you and challenge your preconceptions about the subject.

Access doesn't often come without some negotiation. My agreement with Sorkin was that I could sit in on almost everything he did (network "notes" sessions were off-limits) as long as I gave him the opportunity to declare certain material off-the-record. As it turned out, there was very little negotiation. When Sorkin was on the phone with Stu Bloomberg, the head of ABC TV, he felt uncomfortable with my using anything from Bloomberg's end of the conversation, as did I, since the executive didn't know I was listening in. So I simply summarized Sorkin's side of the conversation, which gave the reader a good indication of Sorkin's mindset.

Once I sat down to write the piece, I tried to give the reader an intimate sense of Sorkin's prickly complexity—showing, not telling, letting you see his intensity and arrogance instead of hearing about it from the all-too-overused anonymous sources writers frequently rely on. And I also found myself focusing on things that had surprised me, that I'd learned from putting in a lot of hours around Sorkin. It was a rich trove of material, which could be shaped into miniature dramatic scenes: how Sorkin had become a coke addict while writing *An American President*, how he used his own conflicts with ABC as fodder for a *Sports Night* episode, how he used his TV scripts to articulate his own views on issues like affirmative action, and how he treated the writers on his own shows as highly paid researchers.

For the end of the piece, I used an especially telling incident—how when Sorkin was first dating his future wife, he took her to see *An American President*, assuming that she would only like him as a person if she liked his writing too. The piece ended with Sorkin saying that he sees himself "as a guy who's better on paper than in real life." Our readers agreed. The letters about the piece were overwhelmingly critical of Sorkin. But as a journalist, I found him a great subject, because he was no cardboard saint—he was just as irritating, overbearing, and compelling as any of the characters that inhabit his TV shows.

Excerpt:
. . . Barely an hour after the run-through, a call comes in from Bloomberg. Sorkin assures the network chief that he's building up the relationship between Dana and Casey—an obvious ABC

priority—and downplays the episode's acerbic shots at network executives. "Stu, you're not the devil," he says cheerfully. "This is fiction."

It can't help matters that the actress playing one of the episode's executives, a pretty woman with a mane of curly hair, bears an obvious resemblance to recently departed ABC Entertainment President Jamie Tarses. "I understand the resemblance, but it's totally coincidental," Sorkin insists. "I wouldn't do that to Jamie. We just thought the actress sounded like a lot of network execs we'd had meetings with."

Still, the point is made: The battles facing the characters in *Sports Night* aren't so different from the ones Sorkin confronts. After talking with Bloomberg, Sorkin launches into a slashing, two-cigarette soliloquy that you could imagine Dana delivering on a future show. "Stu is a good man, and I like his taste, but something is clearly bothering him. He's losing money on our show and he's got a creator-head-writer-executive-producer—me—who's a real pain in the ass. But I care more about pleasing my cast and Tommy than I do the network.

"This isn't TV camp. I see people who don't write or act or direct or carry a sound boom, and yet they're experts on doing a TV show. If you work at ABC and you're insistent that your hands be on the steering wheel of this show, let me ask this—are you the creative inspiration behind *Two Guys, a Girl, and a Pizza Place?* Or behind *Two of a Kind?* Because that's not the person I want on this show."

Sorkin sighs as he lights a new cigarette. "I know that arrogance and belligerence plays a huge part in this, but I want to be liked too, and it'll bother me if Stu thinks I'm a jerk. But if I make an argument against a network idea, I want to hear an intelligent response. Instead, they just run back to their boss and say, 'Hey, Aaron threw a ball at me!' Collaboration is about yelling and debating and standing on sofas. I can't just take the network's notes and fix things. Once that happens, I just become a stenographer. If it gets to that point, hey, I can get a whole lot more money spending a week rewriting a script for Jerry Bruckheimer."

Sorkin exhales a cloud of smoke. "In fact, I still have another television show."

Reporter Matea Gold invoked the show-don't-tell ethic while trying to explain the phenomenon of "language brokers"—children who translate adult-level conversation and written materials for non-English-speaking parents.
Here's how the story started:

Jessica Ramirez already has a pretty busy schedule, what with fifth grade and ballet class and tutoring after school.

But the bright, affectionate girl with lively brown eyes also juggles another set of duties: After school, she sorts through the mail at her Boyle Heights home and goes over the bills with her parents. She marks down appointments and deadlines on the calendar hanging on the kitchen wall. If the phone rings, she jumps to get it. She sits down in the evenings with her younger brother and helps him with his homework. She accompanies her mother everywhere—to the grocery store, doctor's office, teacher's conferences—and stays at her elbow, ready to help explain a product or a medical prescription or her progress in school.

Jessica, 11, is her family's gatekeeper, the main conduit between . . .

What gave the piece its intimacy were the portraits Matea painted from her time hanging out with Jessica's family. Like this:

One recent evening, Jessica and her brother Hugo sat cross-legged on the living room floor, hunched over their homework, their parents watching from the couch.

Hugo, an energetic 6-year-old, furrowed his brow as he tried to read a practice work sheet for the Stanford 9 test.

"How many . . ." He struggled over the next word. His mother looked over his shoulder, trying to decipher what it said. He looked at his mother, then turned to his sister.

"Jessica, can you please tell me what this says?" Hugo asked.

Jessica read it out loud carefully: "How many slides are there at the school and at the park?"

As Dolores watched, the children went through the problems together. She tried to follow along, asking Jessica what the questions meant.

"Is he doing it right?" she asked.

As the two children worked on the photocopied assignment, the mother looked through the papers in Hugo's school folder, a puzzled look on her face.

"It's frustrating," Dolores said. "It makes me feel powerless. I wish I could help him, and it makes me sad that I can't. But I'm happy she can."

Matea elaborates:

I knew that a story about kids who translate for their parents wouldn't resonate unless readers could actually feel what it was like to be young and overwhelmed. Just describing the pressures would be too clinical, too easy to dismiss. The reader had to be in the shoes of that kid who had the burden of interpreting at every turn.

Finding the right family to observe was the tough part. Language brokering is such a matter-of-fact part of life for many families that a lot of children I interviewed couldn't put into words what they did or how it made them feel. Many of them weren't even in a position to understand the impact it had on their lives. I heard a lot of comments like, "I think it's nice because I get to help my mom." But behind that, I knew a lot of children were forced into difficult situations.

This story proved, once again, that it's worth it to invest the time to find that perfect (or near-perfect) source. I interviewed more than 20 kids at schools and community centers before I found Jessica. Even some children who seemed like good candidates lived with an older brother or aunt at home who knew English, and I wanted to find a family representative of the burdens kids take on.

Jessica was one of the students I talked to in a fifth-grade class in Boyle Heights. She was very articulate and although she didn't share any frustrations she felt, something she said caught my attention: "Sometime I just feel like a human dictionary."

I had a long interview with her and her mother at their home one afternoon and they agreed to let me hang out with them. I asked them to think of all the situations in which Jessica translated, and planned my reporting accordingly.

While I was with them one evening, Jessica sat down to help her brother with his homework while her mother sat next to them and watched helplessly. It perfectly illustrated the tensions created by this dynamic. I watched Jessica go through the bills and spent about an hour talking to her about money. Finally, she told me she once had a dream that there was a really big bill she couldn't pay.

That kind of detail is the pay-off from investing the time to really get to know your sources. They don't always know what answer you're looking for, so you have to watch long enough until you see it for yourself.

The last section of the story, capturing a poignant moment, illustrated the pay-off again:

> On one recent Saturday morning, Jessica helped her mother check ingredients and prices at a grocery store a few blocks from their house.
> Then she spotted her friend Monica coming into the store.
> "Monica!" she called, and ran toward her.
> "Jessica, I need you," her mother called after her. "Come back here!"

Jessica nodded as she skipped off. "I'll be right back," she said.

Finally, she dashed back to her mother's cart. But as they shopped, she kept trotting off to find her friend. They giggled and ran up and down the aisles.

At the register, the cashier told Dolores Ramirez to press the green button to approve her credit card purchase.

"Press Enter," the cashier said loudly in English. "You understand?"

The mother nodded, and looked toward Jessica, but the little girl was distracted, talking to her friend. She had slipped back into being 11 years old, momentarily forgetting her responsibilities as a human dictionary.

Alone, the mother paused for a moment, uncertain.

"Si," she finally responded, hoping she was getting it right. "Si."

Chapter 2: The Lead

The Cult of the Fourth Paragraph

You know that feeling you get when you're in a movie theater and you're 20 minutes into the film and you still don't know where the hell the story's going? Now you know what it's like to be a subscriber making his or her way through too many of our anecdotal leads.

Too often, these well-intentioned vehicles—intended to personalize the abstract or the complex—careen off on a tangent, an unnecessary quote, or a contradiction before they fill in the reader on the key question: What is this story about? For all the images and intellectual capital these leads possess, their structure conspires against the reader, and against the newspaper's desire to be quicker to the punch and to say more in less space.

See if you're patient enough to stay with this example:

> Few entrepreneurs go hunting for venture capital while eight months pregnant. But in the land-rush environment of the Internet, expectant mom Laurie McCartney knew she couldn't afford to delay the birth of her online business, EStyle.
>
> Besides, who better to pitch a retail site catering to moms-to-be than its pregnant chief executive? Of course it didn't hurt that McCartney also had a Harvard MBA and strategic planning experience with Walt Disney Co., the big daddy of consumer marketers.
>
> Now armed with $15 million in venture capital, a management team packed with fellow Disney expatriates, an internationally recognized spokesmom in supermodel Cindy Crawford —and McCartney's infant son Jack plugging products on the Web site—L.A.-based EStyle is looking to grow its first-born e-tail store, Babystyle. com, into the premier online site for upscale maternity clothes and baby gear.
>
> "We want to develop an emotional relationship with the consumer," said McCartney, 32. "[Our strategy] is very Disney-esque in that way."
>
> Whether she can emulate the success of her old employer is far from certain. Babystyle isn't the first, the largest, or the cheapest online mom-and-baby store.
>
> What's clear is that a new breed of entrepreneurs such as McCartney—folks who cut their teeth in fields such as entertainment or consumer marketing rather than computer programming—are turning Southern California into one of the most fertile hubs of e-commerce outside Silicon Valley. In the first half

of 1999 alone, venture capitalists invested a record $1. 1 billion in young Southland companies, primarily in Internet start-ups.

In addition to EStyle, this year's venture winners include . . .

The story finally gathered itself—declared itself—in the sixth paragraph, and even there it made you wade through a pair of dashes before the moment occurred. It took 213 words. Be honest: Would you have the patience to wait, with all those other stories on the same page?

The New York Times *can be just as guilty. Try this one on for size:*

On the morning of the 1996 Presidential election, Sharon Denny showered and dressed. She drove to the polling place, an elementary school in her neighborhood in Houston, and on the way she gave herself a pep talk. "This is so important," she told herself. "And it makes such a difference to our country. You have got to go vote."

But standing in line for the voting booth, Ms. Denny, who is 51, grew anxious. What if she got inside and did not know what to do? What if she punched the wrong holes? She broke into a cold sweat, she recalls, and she remembers thinking, "This is why they don't want people with mental illness to vote, because what if I get up there and I really want to vote for Bill Clinton and I don't, I end up voting for Dole?"

Defeated, Ms. Denny, who has suffered from manic-depression for 35 years, returned home, her ballot uncast, as it has been in every election since she first registered to vote 15 years ago.

In next year's Presidential election, however, Ms. Denny knows that she will make it to the front of the line and that she will finally vote for the candidate and the initiatives she believes in.

She is certain of this because in August she joined the Mental Health Voter Empowerment Project, an effort to create a nationwide constituency of people with mental illness by locating potential voters—whether in hospitals, at advocacy events, in housing projects, or support groups—registering them, educating them about mental health issues, and making sure they get to the polls on Election Day 2000.

A volunteer from the project will call to remind Ms. Denny to . . .

It took 220 words, and brought you into the fifth paragraph before you were informed of the existence of the Mental Health Voter Empowerment Project, which is the point of the story. Just as the first example squandered valuable words on secondary details and quotes before revealing itself to us, the voting story committed a couple of unpardonable sins: Like Example 1, it wastes your time on quotes that could have been just as well paraphrased—twice. And, even worse, it turns you in another direction before it turns you toward the point of the story. In graph two, we hit our first "but," which is where you'd expect the anecdote to pivot toward the point of the story. But that won't happen until graph four, where the "however" in the first sentence warns us that the story is turning yet again. Why would a writer want to frustrate an empathetic reader? Why wouldn't her editor say: "Good lead, but it's too fat. You can do it in four graphs instead of five. Just kill the first graph so that the story begins with Ms. Denny inside the Houston voting booth, sweating it out."

Better yet, the editor might have said, "Here's the Wall Street Journal. *Read it for a week and notice that it virtually commands its writers to bring anecdotal leads into focus by the fourth paragraph."*

Sound arbitrary? The Journal *is mocked in some quarters for a formulaic approach to its anecdotal leads, but that's about as valid as complaining that Sam Phillips used a formula because all those Sun Records rockabilly hits of the 1950s were between 2:25 and 2:50 minutes long. In both cases, the trick was letting great ideas unfold creatively within a disciplined setting.*

You can almost set your watch by the efficiency of the Journal's *anecdotal leads. By the fourth paragraph you are into the story and along for the ride. You have sampled great density of detail, or a scene, or a quote—or possibly all three—with commendable efficiency that the previous two examples lacked.*

The following Journal *piece is an e-commerce story that needed only 122 words to get to the point (paragraph four, sentence two):*

> Toby Lenk, founder of eToys Inc., is sure he knows the secret behind e-commerce: Build a single-focus Internet site, laser in on one swath of the marketplace, and don't let customers get confused by clutter from other goods or services.
>
> Jeff Bezos, founder of Amazon. com Inc., is just as confident about his strategy: Build the world's biggest online department store, then offer everything from Milton to modems, so shoppers can get whatever they want with one click on their Web browsers.
>
> Messrs. Lenk and Bezos are true pioneers, Internet innovators with astonishing net worths. So if they're both so shrewd, how could they take such widely disparate gambles?
>
> That question, in one form or another, is on the minds of executives everywhere. In businesses ranging from aerospace to telecommunications, CEOs are making big strategic bets, trying to position their companies to take advantage of productivity and technology trends that they are only beginning to understand. And very often, major players are making completely divergent bets within the same industry.

This example from the Journal *needed only 114 words to do both the set-up and the nut in three graphs:*

BERLIN—As Nick Jackson hawks tickets for his morning walking tour of the city, a Chilean woman approaches, her parents in tow, and spits out three questions in a single breath: "How long is the tour? Do you have senior-citizen discounts? Do you go to see the Wall?"

"Three-and-a-half hours. It's 15 marks [$8] for everyone. And, yes, I'll take you to the Wall," the guide replies. "Not that there's much left," he confides to someone else.

As the Chileans will discover, the Berlin Wall is hard to find in Berlin today. In fact, its remnants are more prominently displayed at Honolulu Community College than in the heart of the city it once divided.

Of the roughly 28 miles of wall that bisected Berlin, less than a mile remains standing, and most of that is in an out-of-the-way . . .

You are also likely to find a stronger writer's voice in many of the Journal's *anecdotal leads than ours, because the* Journal's *devotion to compression forces the writer to employ his own devices rather than the journalese of standard anecdotal leads. Like this one, which took 133 words to get to the point (graph four, sentence two):*

SAN FRANCISCO—There was romance in the resumes: She, a computer consultant turned fashion model; he, an Apple Computer engineer turned Silicon Valley entrepreneur. They were young, beautiful, wired for love.

But caution fell between them. During a yearlong courtship, Alfred Tom held back, wary of revealing too much. Then it happened. After an afternoon with friends, Mr. Tom took Angela Fu back to his car. There, on the front seat of his 1994 Integra, he went for it.

"Naturally, I flinched a bit," Ms. Fu says. But in a stroke it was done: a signed nondisclosure agreement, or NDA, in the parlance of the Net set. Henceforth, Ms. Fu would be sworn to silence about her boyfriend's trade secrets.

DNA, meet NDA, your twisted, alphabetical cousin in the world of baser instincts. Long the province of lawyers, investment bankers, and other traffickers in corporate secrets, nondisclosure agreements have gone mainstream.

Propelled by Internet frenzy, an epidemic of secrecy pacts is . . .

The Journal's *sense of purposefulness is so strong you can usually identify the specific role that each paragraph plays. Try this one, which takes 188 words to get to the point (graph four, sentence two):*

1. Image

HENDERSON, KY.—Tim Hazel, a 23-year-old with bleached-blond hair, a goatee, and five earrings lining his left ear, gazes thoughtfully at a pair of brand new blue jeans. Then he gets down to work, savagely grinding sandpaper across the thighs and knees.

2. Action

With swift strokes, he creates "whiskers" (crease lines near the crotch), "crumples" (three-dimensional whiskers, usually added at the back of the knee) and tears up the hems, waist, and fly. By the time he's done, the pants look like they've been worn by an urban skateboarder who spends most of his time skidding in his jeans across the concrete jungle.

3. Context

Mr. Hazel's boss takes this in approvingly. "Tim's about the best person in the world at making a pair of jeans look worn," says Bart Sights, president of Sights Denim Systems Inc., which is paid by the nation's largest jean manufacturers to take perfectly good blue jeans and beat them up. "It's really an art form."

4. Expanded Context

And an art form in high demand these days. Grunge is hardly a newcomer to fashion circles—faded and stonewashed jeans have been around for more than a decade. But lately, the fashion world's taste in denim has gone true grit, favoring jeans that are frayed, ripped, beat up, and downright dirty.

5. Examples

Designer Calvin Klein made a splash during the New York fashion shows last month by announcing that dirty denim—faux-stained oily and tinted jeans that look like they might have been thrown away by an auto mechanic—would play a major role in his spring line. Now manufacturers and retailers such as . . .

Each paragraph incrementally improved your understanding of how the image in the first graph fit into a broader context. If that's formulaic writing, order me a six-pack of the formula.

Former Journal *editor and writer Bill Blundell puts it this way in* The Art & Craft of Feature Writing, *based on the* Journal's *in-house writing guide: "We do try to engage the reader's attention immediately. We do try to give him a clear idea of what we're up to early on. And we do try to prove our assertions in detail throughout. If these add up to a formula then I suppose we have one. But it offers the reporter enormous latitude, and it's the same one successful storytellers have used for centuries."*

So beat yourself up a little more. Be more purposeful, more unforgiving of your tangents. Play a game with yourself: Draw the line at four graphs per anecdotal lead—and that includes the graph that tells the reader what the story's about. See whether it forces you into some positive habits—better distillation, better use of your own voice as a writer, a stronger sense of urgency in your work, and greater clarity.

Dependent Clauses: Keep 'Em in Check

In an effort to create a debate on a significant grammatical issue that appears to bedevil many newspaper writers, I would like to undertake a discussion of overwritten dependent clauses.

We've all been forced to wade through leads like that, in which the writer— determined to simultaneously proclaim the news and put it into perspective— creates one big fat impenetrable sentence. The previous paragraph, for example, was a sentence in which 19 of the 31 words—59 percent—consisted of the dependent clause.

Newspapers, like parking lots, do not have a lot of rules that work consistently, and dependent clauses are no exception. But we clearly publish too many that put too much weight on the remainder of the sentence and crush its meaning. We need to develop a more disciplined, leaner style that concentrates on moving the reader from one reasoned, shorter sentence to the next.

The biggest reason you keep seeing monster dependent clauses choking off sentence logic is the writer's (or editor's) insecurity: Rather than wait until the second or third paragraph to explain perspective, the writer fears you'll abandon him unless he shoves it down your throat right now. Think about it: If you don't trust the reader to follow a straightforward, one- or two-sentence lead to the second or third paragraph, you've got bigger problems.

Evaluate your own habits and standards as you read the following examples. The length of the dependent clause increases with each one.

11 words, *34 percent of the sentence: Here's an acceptable and necessary use of a dependent clause. The contrast between the information in the dependent clause and the independent clause is a moral hub of the investigation:*

> At a time when improving America's schools is a government priority, Congress has increasingly been raiding the money

set aside for education reform to pay for pet projects, records and interviews show.

In the current federal budget, lawmakers have dipped into national education money to finance perks for their home districts, honor retired colleagues and help well-connected constituents.

Congress "went hog wild" bestowing such benefits, said . . .

13 words, *31 percent of the sentence: The ratio is acceptable but it makes too long a sentence. More important, how genuinely important is the contrast the writer tries to illustrate? He doesn't immediately return to it, so why jam it so high?*

Even as they searched for a speedy, bipartisan resolution to the impeachment crisis, senators from both parties urged President Clinton on Sunday to postpone his Jan. 19 State of the Union address because the Senate may be debating whether to remove him from office.

The extraordinary suggestion, made by several participants in televised talk shows, signals a growing recognition that the impeachment trial will inevitably slow, if not stop, Washington from conducting the public's routine business. In his annual State of the Union address, which is delivered to a joint session of Congress, the president traditionally . . .

Now go back and draw a line through the dependent clause and read the lead without it. See what you think.

20 words, *54 percent of the sentence: This story succeeds in cramming the two key developments into one sentence. But it's confusing when you hit the word "his" before you figure out who the protagonist is:*

Minutes after filing a federal civil-rights complaint demanding a review of the fatal police shooting of his 19-year-old cousin, a Riverside pastor Monday implored several hundred protesters to seek justice peacefully.

The boisterous, incident-free rally was led by local ministers and community activists—including members of the victim's family. Some of the placards waved by protesters read "Murdered by the Riverside Police," "Guns don't kill, Cops do," and "Help! 911 Killed Me."

"We're not seeking the path of violence," shouted the Rev. DeWayne Butler, a cousin and father-figure of the victim, Tyisha Miler.

It would be clearer (albeit still long-winded) to say:

> A Riverside pastor on Monday filed a federal civil-rights complaint demanding a review of the fatal police shooting of his 19-year-old cousin, then implored several hundred protesters to seek justice peacefully.
> The boisterous, incident-free rally . . .

22 words, *54 percent of the sentence: In this story the technology is esoteric, so the factors that have propelled its rise should have taken second place to the rise itself. The story tried to have it both ways:*

> Propelled by the introduction of broadcast digital television in the top U.S. markets last fall and the coming of digital cable systems, interactive TV is poised to move from regional experiments into living rooms across the nation this year.
> Products and services that allow consumers to personalize their TV experience will provide much of the buzz at this week's Consumer Electronics Show in Las Vegas. CES will see a raft of announcements by software and hardware suppliers racing to form partnerships and release interactive-TV products.
> Interactive-TV services allow viewers to use their remote controls or wireless keyboards to get more information during a broadcast or to treat their TVs somewhat like a substitute computer monitor to get e-mail and surf the Web. For example, a viewer might be able to get profiles of players while watching a soccer match by pressing a button on the remote.
> Set to debut this year are TVs with software built in that allow viewers to interact with . . .

Suggestion: Lower the perspective. Make it the fourth paragraph (shown underlined) or, if you think the perspective is more important than the definition, the third:

> Interactive TV is poised to move from regional experiments into living rooms across the nation this year.
> Products and services that allow consumers to personalize their TV experience will provide much of the buzz at this week's Consumer Electronics Show in Las Vegas. CES will see a raft of announcements by software and hardware suppliers racing to form partnerships and release interactive-TV products.
> Interactive-TV services allow viewers to use their remote controls or wireless keyboards to get more information during a

broadcast or to treat their TVs somewhat like a substitute computer monitor to get e-mail and surf the Web. For example, a viewer might be able to get profiles of players while watching a soccer match by pressing a button on the remote.

The technology's popularity has been propelled by the introduction of broadcast digital television in the top U.S. markets last fall and the coming of digital cable systems.

Set to debut this year are TVs with software built in that allow viewers to interact with . . .

Chapter 3: Sequencing

Prewriting: Talk It Out First

Sportswriter David Wharton was ready to write a piece that felt cinematic, shifting from New York to New Mexico and concluding in L.A. It was the story of a USC basketball player who came from a poor New York background, and a woman in New Mexico who salvaged him. In preparing to write the piece, David went to a book on film technique for inspiration. Before he talks about what he learned, read the top sections of his story:

> The trip from New Mexico takes seven hours of driving, flying, then more driving. She comes every other week to watch a young and struggling USC basketball team.
>
> "Her?" an usher at the Sports Arena asks. "That woman is in her own world."
>
> Diane Taylor stands just under five feet tall. She is middle-aged and suitably dressed, a gold cross hanging from a gold chain around her neck. She always sits behind the bench and everyone knows her by the odd-looking stick she carries.
>
> The size of a cane, it is covered with bells and bangles, and there is a cymbal attached on top. It is the kind of contraption a fan might rattle after dunks and three-point baskets.
>
> "My boombah," she calls it. And once the game begins, Taylor pounds that stick.
>
> She pounds it on the floor, hard enough to startle people sitting nearby. She pounds it for reasons that have little to do with basketball.
>
> People wonder about that woman.

From there, the story moves to the other protagonist, the player:

> His voice settles between a whisper and a growl, his eyes half-lidded, as he tells his story. Elias Ayuso starts long ago, long before he became a sharpshooting guard for the Trojans, running the court with the jangle of the boombah in his ears. He was 8 when he left Puerto Rico with his mother and brothers and sisters, on their way to becoming another immigrant family in the South Bronx.
>
> "The guy who lived below us, he had some problems with drug stuff," Ayuso says. "I don't know if he owed money or what but they wanted to kill him. They threw a firebomb into his apartment."

It was late at night and Ayuso was watching television with his family.

"The hallway was nothing but smoke," he says. "We couldn't take the fire escape so we got everybody and we covered my little brother's mouth and we just ran down the steps."

They lost everything. People from the next building brought out old clothes but the best they could find for Ayuso was a blouse and baggy pants.

"They dressed me in girlie clothes," he says.

The next few years, as his family drifted through shelters and low-rent hotels . . .

The second section ends with Ayuso drifting into trouble, and then proceeds to the third section, the logical narrative in which Taylor and Ayuso intersect:

What does it take to save a kid? What can salvage a child who learns to connive and brawl the way other children learn to brush their teeth and do their homework? Before Taylor tries to answer the question, she has a story of her own to tell.

It goes back to a Pennsylvania mining town called Carbondale, where she was a little girl from an Irish-Italian family as big as it was poor. There wasn't money for a doctor's visit when she fell ill and she recalls coughing so loudly on the street that two well-dressed women stopped to watch.

"Go home," one of them said. "You're disgusting."

Decades later, the 49-year-old woman clenches her hand into a fist and says, "I remember thinking that no one would ever treat me that way again."

The memory made her tough as nails, fiery as her red hair. It . . .

Eventually, Ayuso winds up in the New Mexico town where Taylor has settled. The story describes how she helps him get to USC and continues her commitment to him.

Here's Dave:

Some stories require no nut graph or statistics, no quotes from experts. They are tales, pure and simple. The moment I heard about Elias Ayuso, I figured he'd make for that kind of story. As a teen, Ayuso robbed and stole on the Bronx streets. When his brother and friends were killed, he got scared and talked his way into a program that sent him to a foster family in New Mexico. He saw it as a way to stay safe, nothing more. But he ran into a feisty woman who set about trying to change him.

As I gathered information for this yarn, I found myself telling it to colleagues in the office and friends around the dinner table. And that was how I decided to write the piece, as a blend of oral and written storytelling. I then stole a trick from scriptwriting guru Robert McKee.

In his book *Story*, McKee suggests writers outline their screenplays step by step, each scene briefly described on its own index card. With the outline complete, the writer tests his idea by sitting down with a willing listener and reading it aloud.

We've probably all done this with full drafts of articles, but his exercise comes much earlier in the process. "If a story can't work in 10 minutes, how will it work in 110 minutes?" McKee writes. "It won't get better when it gets bigger. Everything that's wrong with a ten-minute pitch is ten times worse on-screen."

His method is, of course, far more involved. He has theories on what makes for a good scene and how stories should progress, all of which makes his book worth buying, even for writers, such as me, with no intentions of attempting a screenplay. But for the purposes of the Ayuso story, I focused on the act of testing my outline.

In many ways, it was the same as reading a draft. When the story moved, my words snapped one after another. When the narrative lagged, I felt uneasy. My kind listener was there to reinforce these perceptions, to tell me which parts of the tale interested him most or not at all.

At the end of an hour (my first try, it went a little long) I had a feel for my priorities. I had a grasp on the story early enough to direct both the reporting and the writing.

I'm not sure the exercise translates to articles on issues or institutions, but it sure helped with a good old-fashioned tale.

Altering Your Sentence Rhythm

Sports columnist Bill Plaschke makes great choices on what to write about, as typified by his recent piece on a Crenshaw High basketball player, and tells his tales with an evocative style. Part of his technique is radically varying the length of his sentences. Here's the first half of that Crenshaw column with the length of each sentence shown in bold type. Listen to the effect:

20— From the moment he stepped into that foreboding land between Slauson and Vernon, David Meriwether just knew people would point.

7— He just knew there would be stomping.

7— He just knew there would be chants.

22— Monday afternoon, amid the dusty haze of history that hangs thick in the legendary Crenshaw High gym, David Meriwether was proven right.

2— And wrong.

24— When he was introduced as a junior guard for the Crenshaw High basketball team before the first official practice, more than 1,000 students pointed.

7— While cheering and whooping and high-fiving.

19— When he ran to the court to join the state's most celebrated high school basketball program, there was stomping.

6— As everyone danced on the bleachers.

18— And yes, by the time he walked into the blue-and-gold embrace of teammates, there were chants:

4— "Milk! Milk! Milk! Milk!"

26— Leave it to a bunch of silly teenagers to compose the perfect nickname for this rich, refreshing break from our city's tired sirens of conflict.

16— Meet David Meriwether, the first white male basketball player in the 30-year history of Crenshaw High.

8— The students have, and they overwhelmingly accept him.

7— His teammates have, and they like him.

13— The coach has, and he thinks Meriwether has a chance to be good.

29— "This is cool," Meriwether said Monday, bouncing off the shoulders of buddies, posing for giggling girls, looking at home in a place as foreign to most whites as Mars.

2— Yeah. Cool.

26— To understand the importance of the enrollment of a single student in a high school of about 2,760, it should be understood who doesn't enroll here.

2— Whites don't.

13— You can literally count the number of them at Crenshaw High on one hand.

4— David Meriwether makes four.

21— During his first two weeks of school, he was consistently bumped in the halls by gang members and questioned by classmates.

Ask Bill what he's trying to accomplish, and here's his answer:

Like many journalists, while I report with my eyes, I write with my ears. One way I attempt to keep a good rhythm is to vary the length of my sentences.

Sometimes, as crazy as it sounds, it's as if I try to turn my 25-inch story into a drumbeat. Looooong sentence. Short. Short. Looooong sentence. Short. Short. It's never that structured, of course. But that's sometimes how it works out.

I think in these weird terms because I always read my stories aloud to myself as I'm doing the final edit before I send them in. I want them to "sound" interesting.

Most of us would agree that one long-winded discourse after another is not interesting, whether you are hearing it on a podium or at a party. I'm thinking, why should it be different in a story?

I don't think this means you also have to break up those sentences into different paragraphs, the sort of one- and two-word graphs my readers have chided me about. Sometimes I think I use my short paragraphs as a crutch, relying on typography to provide drama that my writing may lack.

You can vary sentence length within long paragraphs and, for me, it's just as effective. As long as I keep the beat.

Normal stories often can't sustain such radical changes in pace, but even if you throw the reader just one change-up within a single story, it gives the writing more power.

Consider the following paragraph from the middle of a recent story about a Marine shot to death at a bus stop while home on leave. (The words-per-sentence cadence, for those keeping score, is 7/4/4/22/6/3/7.):

There, Giovanni exchanged stares with another teenager. Glowering led to words. Words led to punches. Giovanni had the upper hand, witnesses told police, when his opponent backed away and reached for a zippered binder he was carrying. His hand emerged with a gun. He fired once. Giovanni crumpled to the sidewalk, mortally wounded.

Why Ideas Always Overpower Wordplay

It wasn't only that it was a tidy 36 inches. It wasn't only that it came racing out of the gate, grabbed you by the throat, and never slowed down. It wasn't only that just

93 of its 1,265 words were in quotations. It wasn't only that it found an intriguing nexus of two subjects we rarely put together—commerce and culture. It was the fact that all of those things occurred within one story: Mark Magnier's page 1 feature about Japan's fascination with high-tech toilets.

By being smart, taut, and original, the story relied on the power of ideas rather than the cuter, slower, more self-indulgent style of wordplay that too often makes the Times *sluggish and alienating to read. It's a choice we need to make more often.*

Mark's story, and two other page 1 features published during the following three days, were marked by a writer's enthusiasm communicated not by adverbs or adjectives or asides, but by a more direct, stripped-down rush of information—a pure need to tell a story. Paralleling this enthusiasm was a sense of purpose and a sense of seriousness—a grown-up way of storytelling that gave the reader credit for his intelligence and endeavored to tell him something he didn't know.

None of the three stories were projects or stories with literary aspirations; they were meat-and-potato enterprise features (averaging 48 inches), the kind everyone on every beat should be shooting for.

One test should be a devotion to stripping out writing that tells more about the writer than the story. Another should be getting rid of soft or overlapping quotations. Both of those standards need to be applied so that we can discover a higher kind of stylishness, a writing voice that shows off by not showing off. We are inconsistent at doing this, and yet there are many models to choose from and to steal from.

Consider this trio, starting with Mark's, told almost exclusively in Mark's voice. The first 11 graphs had no quotes. Same for an even longer middle stretch— graphs 13 through 27. It began:

> KOKURA, JAPAN—It's got wings, it's sensitive, it's smart. It cares, it knows when you're around, it bleats when you arrive. Ignore it and you could be sorry. Treat it well and it will comfort you in your old age.
>
> A new kind of house pet? No, it's the Japanese toilet in all its glory. And if you believe its makers, it's only getting better.

After those two graphs of engagement, the payoff:

> Japan has an enduring fascination with the toilet, replete with cutting-edge intelligent-toilet research, toilet Web sites, symposiums, antique toilet museums, solid 24-karat-gold johns, and official Toilet Days. Nowhere else on Earth do so many people spend so much money on such expensive thrones.

Then the global/cultural perspective:

> Japan's enthusiasm is largely lost on foreigners. In sharp contrast to their receptiveness to the Japanese cameras, autos,

and Walkmans that have taken the world by storm, few Americans or Europeans seem to covet Japan's super bowls—some of which can cost $4,000.

Then what's new:

Now major Japanese manufacturers hope to change that by creating something with more universal appeal. Their latest project: a toilet that doubles as a doctor's office.

At Matsushita's research center in Tokyo, scientists explain how they are working on embedding technology in the porcelain that will catch a urine sample, shoot it full of lasers, and in short order test it for glucose, kidney disease and eventually even cancer.

One of the researchers, Tatsuro Kawamura, says future smart toilets will compile and compare medical results day by day, allowing doctors to spot important changes.

Now, the story focuses in on one company:

Japan's undisputed king of toilets is Toto Ltd., which has noticed the enormous profits ahead in serving Japan's rapidly aging population, although it's moving slower on the medical front.

Toto set the industry standard in the 1980s with its high-tech Washlet, which got worldwide publicity at the time. With the slogan "Even your bottom wants to stay clean," it built mass appeal in Japan for the $1,000-and-up toilets previously confined to sanitariums and hospitals.

Nearly 20 years later, these once-luxury items can be found in about 30% of Japanese homes. The fully configured Washlet, the Lexus of toiletry, has enough lights, hoses, buttons, remote controls, and temperature and water-pressure adjustments to bowl over even the most avid gadget freak.

Master the Washlet's controls—many foreigners don't and emerge soaking and embarrassed—and your bum will be warmed even as your undercarriage is squirted with warm water and blow-dried, obviating the need for toilet paper.

Miss your quotes yet? The first one followed:

"Once you use it, you wonder how you could ever do without it," says Mariko Fujiwara, a researcher with the Hakuhodo Institute of Life and Living.

And then Mark went back to the races:

> What's behind Japan's keen interest in toiletry?
> Takahiko Furata, director of Aomori University's. . . .

When I complimented Mark, he credited his editor, Don Woutat, with shaping the story. Natch, there were painful trims: "One big chunk that we decided to cut was a history of toilets down through the centuries," Mark said. "The museum is housed in Toto's headquarters and shows a toilet timeline dating back to Mesopotamia. In the end, though, we decided to be ruthless to keep things more concise and focused."

Two days after Mark's story ran, John Daniszewski of our Cairo bureau did the same thing: a 51-inch story that was only 8 percent quotes profiling the ruler of Oman, who had transformed his country from a Middle Ages relic. The writer was confident enough to not use a quote—even though this was a profile—until the six-teenth graph. The middle of the story contains two ten-graph sections with no quotes.

Where Mark had used a mock sales-pitch voice, John modeled his after what might have been a desert fantasy:

> MUSCAT, OMAN—There once was a boy who was shunned by his wealthy and powerful father. He was sent to a foreign land to be educated. To support himself, he had to join a foreign army. When at last his father sent for him, the young man hurried home full of expectations—only to learn he was to be kept out of sight.
>
> It was an unpromising beginning to an Arabian tale, but it has had a happy ending for the boy, now known as Sultan Kaboos ibn Said, supreme ruler of the Sultanate of Oman, and es-pecially for his 1.7 million people.

Having engaged the reader, John proclaimed the story simply:

> There are few countries in the world that have come so far so fast under the rule of one man.
>
> At a time when many people think of the Middle East as unsafe, prone to violence, discriminatory toward women and mi-norities, chaotic, and backward, Oman presents an opposite pic-ture. It is clean, pleasant, stable, progressive. It prides itself on creating opportunity for all its citizens.

Then, how it happened:

> This has much to do with Kaboos, who in 1970 deposed his father, Said ibn Taimur, in a bloodless coup aided by relatives

conspiring with the British army. His father was tied to a stretcher and put on a plane for London. And Kaboos went straight to work letting fresh air into what previously had been known as the hermit kingdom of the Middle East.

Most of us would have stopped and inserted a quote, perhaps to express how drastic the change was. John used detail to say it better:

> Three decades ago, the customs of Oman harked back to the Middle Ages. The wooden gates to Muscat, the capital, were closed each night to keep out intruders, and anyone walking about in the darkness (there was no electricity) was required by law to carry a lantern or risk being shot as a thief by city guards. The country had only three miles of paved road and 12 telephones.
>
> Today, Oman is a paragon of development—webbed by thousands of miles of highways, linked to the rest of the globe by the Internet and cellular telephones, open to commerce and tourism, and building one of the largest container ports in the world to take advantage of its location on the world's main east-west shipping lanes.
>
> It also is one of the most tolerant countries in its region. The sultan himself has built churches and a Hindu temple for the Christian and Indian minorities amid the overwhelming Muslim majority. He has spearheaded the cause of women's rights, admitting women to his Consultative Council and allowing them to serve as deputy ministers, a first for any government in the Persian Gulf. He also appointed the first female ambassador from an Arab gulf country.
>
> It is rare on the eve of the 21st century for a traditional monarch to rule a state absolutely. The idea of a hereditary autocrat deciding what's best for a people began to go out of fashion in Europe more than 200 years ago.
>
> But the 59-year-old Kaboos . . .

I still didn't miss my quotes because I was enjoying the way the greater idea—the difference between then and now—was being played out. This is offered not as a diatribe against quotes, but rather as a plea for better reporting that gives the writer enough confidence to make the reader experience the story the same way he did. That is a higher writing value, by and for grown-ups.

The day after John's story ran, higher-education writer Ken Weiss took a potential eyes-glazed-over subject—the UC system in the post-afffirmative-action era—and made you pay attention. You know that cliché about putting the reader in the subject's shoes? Ken did it by speaking to the reader in the second person, instantly achieving a conversational style to make an abstract topic accessible:

> Interested in reading some good sob stories? Try sitting in the chair of an admissions officer on any of the University of California campuses.
>
> There's the essay written by an aspiring UC Berkeley student whose family home and possessions were turned to ashes by a wildfire—everything except her dad's Berkeley class ring. Or the one from a UCLA hopeful whose grades dipped while she worried about her girlfriend's drug problem.
>
> And then there are the deaths of beloved grandfathers. Hundreds of them.
>
> "If you believe these essays, California is the most unhealthy state in the union," said Rae Lee Siporin, UCLA's director of undergraduate admissions. "There are more sick parents. There are more dying grandparents. There are more burned down houses and natural disasters than anywhere else in the world. That is what we hear about over and over again."

The quote worked because the speaker used vivid language that expanded upon the theme of absurdity that Ken had unveiled. Ken then leads you to the heart of the story:

> But if UC officials are tired of these stories, they only have themselves to blame. They asked for them.
>
> No longer able to consider race or gender in picking the freshman class, the officials are trying another approach to maintain diversity in their student body: "We are really looking for kids who have achieved something in the face of obstacles," said UC Berkeley Chancellor Robert M. Berdahl. "'We just can't take race into account as one of the obstacles."

The middle of the story did a good job of using interpretive language to put the "hardship" con game into a social context with passages like:

> Perhaps no other piece of writing carries such weight in determining one's destiny. Living in a material world, teenagers are suddenly supposed to turn introspective and spill their guts on paper in a way that will sum up their accomplishments, demonstrate their maturity, and perhaps even show a flair for writing—all in a couple of pages.

And, later:

Tugging on the heartstrings of college admissions officers comes naturally for many students. They know these stories sell. After all, they are bombarded with them at the movies, on television and sports pages: The hero or heroine must surmount daunting hurdles—or suffer through a life-shattering event— before emerging as the champion or the queen of the ball.

In an example of art imitating life imitating art, the hip television writers on the hit show *Felicity* explored the trend of fudged tragedies. Felicity, the show's namesake character who developed a crush on a boy and followed him to a New York university, secretly reads his application essay while working part-time for the university. He had written a three-hankie tale about his older brother, who died of brain cancer. The problem was, as she later discovers, he never had a brother.

The command these three writers exerted allowed them to say more with relatively little room. They were tough enough to say no to tangents, a distraction that is too often brought on us by both writers (who worked hard to find the information and are determined to jam it in) and editors (who imagine a reader asking a question that few normal readers would consider).

Chapter 5: The Perspective Paragraph

Don't Make Your Readers Extrapolate

Pretend you're an ordinary reader. This means you are an inconsistent reader. Stories build and you don't always catch the initial progressions. It may not be until a story bounces onto A-1, or the top of a section's front page, that you say to yourself, "I guess I better check this out and improve my hazy understanding."

It's at that point that you appreciate a boilerplate perspective paragraph that clues you in on why this running story has been running as long as it has— information that is a "given" to the reporter or editor, or to the best-informed reader, but remains vital to bring all readers up to speed, giving them quick context to appreciate the new developments.

Obvious? Consider two examples from Dec. 1, 1999, as cautionary tales.

The first was the A-1 story about protests in Seattle on the first day of the World Trade Organization meeting in Seattle. It captured the color and rage of the unusually large demonstrations, but did not attempt to explain until the nineteenth graph—far into the jump—why the protests were happening. What the hell was it about the WTO—an organization that many readers could easily have ignored until the protest story—that angered so many people? Before the jump, an accompanying A-1 sidebar elliptically alluded to a wide array of groups linked against "the faceless forces of globalization," but that wouldn't take a casual reader very far. Even when the mainbar finally addressed the reason for the protest, it did so in a fragmentary way, with details littered in graphs 19 through 23, forcing you to add up the nature of the protesters and their causes.

By contrast, the New York Times *clued you in by the third paragraph of its Dec. 1 mainbar. After a second paragraph explained how WTO members had expected the meeting to be a crowning success for the global economy, the third graph said:*

> But the protesters have descended on Seattle with an eclectic array of grievances, most centered around the sentiment that the trade organization is a handmaiden of corporate interests whose rulings undermine health, labor, and environmental protections around the world

We weren't alone in treating a complex explanation as a "given." When the Associated Press moved a follow-up story the morning of Dec. 2, it wasn't until the seventeenth paragraph that it clued the ordinary reader by saying:

> Some of the more moderate opponents want the WTO to include tougher labor and environmental standards in any trade deal—an idea strongly opposed by developing nations in Asia

and Latin America that depend on cheap labor to make economic gains.

Writing that perspective paragraph was harder than it looked. The protesters were a confusing and contradictory bunch, and included some whose bent was naked anarchy. ("A bewildering spectrum of voices," USA Today *said in its Dec. 2 coverage. "Their causes are as varied as food safety, affordable medicine, human rights, clean air, native cultures, and the preservation of species. . . . They are united by a disgust with the WTO, which they see as the tyrannical symbol of a global economy that has shoved social priorities aside in a relentless quest for profits," the* L.A. Times *said in a Dec. 3 sidebar.) The mix of causes was hard to measure and distill, just as we had trouble during the 1992 L.A. riots in establishing different motivations for demonstrators, rioters, and looters. But that muddiness should have been part of the perspective; what we don't know is often as enlightening to the reader as what we do know. Sidestepping or obfuscating the nature of the protests inadvertently made the paper seem arrogant and elitist to many ordinary readers. It forced them to extrapolate—to work too hard.*

Example 2 was found on the same day's sports page. It led with the running story about who's to blame for the Dodgers signing of third-baseman Adrian Beltre before he was of legal age. The controversy centers on whether the Dodgers knowingly violated baseball's rules or were misled by Beltre, who is now a starting infielder. But do you know why that matters? Do you think all of our casual sports fans do? How did they feel when:

1. *They weren't told until the ninth graph that:*

    Boras [Beltre's agent] wants the commissioner's office to grant Beltre free agency because of the Dodgers' alleged violation.

2. *They weren't told until the twentieth graph that:*

    . . . [Beltre] earned $220,000 last season, and the Dodgers planned to increase his salary to about $300,000 next season. If Beltre is granted free agency, he might move among the highest-paid players at his position in the game.

Those paragraphs were the only places in the story where the casual sports reader was given even a chance to combine those two distant paragraphs in order to realize that this running controversy matters hugely: Either the Dodgers will have to pay millions more to keep Beltre or they will lose him to another team willing to pay even more.

Wouldn't it have made more sense to inject a boilerplate sentence somewhere in the first five or six graphs to make sure the story appealed to a broader audience? The informed readers wouldn't have minded; they would have recognized the contextual device and breezed right by it.

Think about this quandary next time you're writing a multiprogression story: Have mercy on the ordinary reader.

Chapter 6: Your Inner Voice

The Power of a True News Analysis

For beat reporters, another way of taking command of the facts is to use the expertise that is too often hidden behind standard journalese. Our assignment editors should be pushing their beat reporters harder for news analyses that give the reader a better explanation of how the world works. Too often, our news analyses fall back on presenting the consensus of experts rather than offering an independent observation. If you're looking for a model of a stronger intellect at work, pull up some of the news analyses by Maura Reynolds in our Moscow bureau. What's striking is her willingness to be assertive, and to use "experts" merely as occasional supplemental instruments; there is no doubt she is fronting the band, as in this news analysis, published two days after Boris Yeltsin resigned, leaving the future of democracy in Russia an open question:

MOSCOW—Russian President Boris N. Yeltsin's resignation speech was filled with fine words, but "democracy" wasn't one of them.

In fact, while he referred four times to the constitution and six times to national elections, Yeltsin made no mention Friday of what the constitution and elections are supposed to bring: participatory democracy in which the will of the people determines who rules.

The omission is telling because Western observers usually credit Yeltsin with bringing at least an elementary democracy to Russia during his eight years in power, listing it near the top of his achievements.

But in Yeltsin's own words, what he accomplished as president was to create "a vital precedent for a civilized and voluntary transfer of power from one president of Russia to another, newly elected one."

Which raises the question: Is this transfer of power, in addition to being voluntary and civilized, also "democratic"?

Yeltsin's supporters would say yes. They point to Russia's regular elections, to the fact that ballots have multiple candidates. and that since the fall of the Soviet Union, Russia has built many of the institutions needed for democracy.

But Pavel I. Voshchanov, a former Yeltsin press secretary, points out that although Russia got a new president Friday, power hasn't really changed hands.

Acting President Vladimir V. Putin was picked and groomed and promoted by the same set of Kremlin power brokers who have stood behind Yeltsin. Known popularly as "The Family," they include Yeltsin's daughter Tatyana Dyachenko, media tycoon Boris A. Berezovsky, and Yeltsin chief of staff Alexander S. Voloshin. One of Putin's first moves as acting president was to name Voloshin his own chief of staff.

"The Yeltsin epoch isn't over yet," Voshchanov said. "The people who are loyal to him are still in power. The Family is still in charge. And they have no intention of ceding the reins of power to anyone else."

Some might even ask whether the Kremlin has, in fact, hijacked the democratic process.

Kremlin leaders would defend themselves on legal grounds. They stress, as Putin did in his first address to the nation, that Yeltsin has scrupulously followed the current constitution. In an interview with Echo Moscow radio, Constitutional Court Judge Nikolai Vedernikov went so far as to proclaim Yeltsin's resignation and hand-over of power "legally pure."

Certainly, Russia has the constitutional and electoral procedures needed for democracy. But when analysts evaluate their outcome, it becomes harder to call Russia's political system a true democracy.

For one thing, constitutionality and democracy are not the same thing. Soviet dictator Josef Stalin was also scrupulous about his constitution . . .

Where do you draw the line? How far do you push beyond standard interpretive reporting until you create a news analysis? How much farther can you push without venturing into the netherworld of an opinion piece? Maura's boss, Simon Li, says he lives by a 1938 pronouncement by CBS news exec Ed Klauber:

What news analysts are entitled to do and should do is to elucidate and illuminate the news out of common knowledge, or special knowledge possessed by them or made available to them by this organization through its sources. They should point out the facts on both sides, show contradictions with the known record, and so on. They should bear in mind that in a democracy it is important that people not only should know but should understand, and it is the analyst's function to help the listener to understand, to weigh, and to judge, but not to do the judging for him.

Maura looks at it this way:

For me, writing an analysis is very personal. I often remind myself that I'm the most important analyst in the story. It can be useful to quote newsmakers and motley experts, but ultimately, an analysis needs a guiding mind. I have access to information and experiences unavailable to the reader, and it's my job to draw on them.

What I try to do is imagine the family and friends who have read my recent news stories and are wondering how to make sense of them. I can't tell them what to think, but I can offer them some ideas about how to think.

I don't think it's a matter of being smart or clever. I think we reporters often fail to appreciate just how much we know about the people and places we cover. I'm often amazed that what to me seems to be a simple observation is to others a profound insight. In fact, when I'm writing an analysis, I often feel like I'm simply stating the obvious. But what's obvious to me is not obvious to the reader.

I find it's often helpful to zero in on an irony or contradiction—something that will intrigue the reader and launch the rest of the piece. That's also a way to write a story that makes an argument without writing a story that takes a side. It never hurts to challenge conventional wisdoms; by the time they become conventional, they aren't usually very wise.

I also think it's important that an analysis have a sense of direction. If it is too much of an "on-one-hand, on-the-other-hand" laundry list of other people's opinions, I think readers feel they are spinning in circles and wind up where they started. I think they appreciate a writer who is going to lead them along a new line of thought and point out things they wouldn't have seen on their own.

I think the reader wants to be challenged, to feel that the writer is engaging them and thinks they are smart enough to appreciate what's behind the news. They don't want to be told what to think, but they do want to come away with something more to think about.

Ultimately, I think it helps to feel comfortable with the difference between analysis and opinion. In American journalism, reporters rightfully don't take sides in debates or promote certain points of view to the detriment of others. But I don't think that means we can't share our thoughts. In fact, given our privileged access to information, I'd argue that we have a responsibility to do so.

Chapter 7: Tapping the Right Brain

Finding the Emotional Truth

> "Newspapers get in trouble when they have a fear . . . of being emotional. . . . Does it mean writing in a way to make the reader care more? You bet."
>
> —Former *Times* publisher Mark Willes in a newspaper interview

When Willes raised this issue in a contentious staff meeting in 1999 it appeared to get lost in a regrettable debate over whether the technique worked better with male or female readers. Let's put that aside and simply chew on what it means to write with more emotion.

The poorest examples are the most literal—the ones in which the writer takes an emotional, bathetic tone. We call this overwriting and we scoff at it because we know the reader sees through it and, ultimately, tires of it.

Truly appealing to a reader's emotional core—finding and exploiting the emotional truth of a story—is something far fewer writers do. Journalism conspires to make us afraid of it—afraid, for example, to flatly proclaim observable or historical truths. Or afraid to exploit the pure narrative potential of a story on those rare occasions when we could actually withhold the conclusion until the end in order to achieve a dramatic effect.

One reason this happens is that although writing is a verbal process, reporting is often nonverbal—it's hard to find the right words for some of the most magical connections or impulses you feel in the field or on the phone when a story is coming together. It's hard to find the right words to pull these truths out of your gut. Too many of us give up, saying with a shrug: "Aw, that's just my opinion, anyway." But often those impulses can be the deeper truths of your story, the places you need to make your story explore.

Let's look at a few of the technical qualities that lie behind effective "emotional" writing: understanding your story, having the guts to proclaim what matters, and creating a theme that matches what you felt while you were reporting. What follows is the beginning of a Sunday Magazine profile, but the tricks are universal.

1. The writer sets the scene with a complication (two graphs):

The speaker is late. Southwest Airlines has deposited him in Burbank way behind schedule and now the whole damn evening is on the cusp of collapse. As he plows through the crowded terminal, 300 people are settling into auditorium seats over on L.A.'s Westside, where he is due to hold forth at some highbrow forum titled "Visions for the New Millennium." The event begins in 24 minutes. The drive from Burbank will take twice that, at best.

Hopping into his black Ford Explorer, the speaker peeks hopefully at his watch. "I hate to be late," he says. "I hate it, I hate it, I hate it."

2. The writer creates a second complication:

His problems don't end there. Foraging through his brief-case, the speaker cannot find his speech. "Visions" is a big-time affair—prominent spectators, TV coverage, hefty topics. He has just become czar of the California State Assembly, and he knows that first impressions count. He wants—and wants very badly—to come off as accomplished, poised. The missing speech is no small concern.

3. The writer shows how attempting to solve the second problem causes a revealing third problem:

He picks up the car phone and dials his Capitol office.

SPEAKER: Get me Zeiger, please.

RECEPTIONIST: Who's calling?

SPEAKER: It's me, Antonio Villaraigosa.

RECEPTIONIST: Uh, I'm sorry, who's calling?

The speaker's broad brow stiffens, a flash of exasperation shadows his youthful face. He repeats his name, insistently now, but it's no use.

RECEPTIONIST: No, really, who is this?

4. The writer reveals how that third complication is a metaphor for the protagonist's existence (three paragraphs):

His name is Antonio Villaraigosa, and if you have never heard of him, you are not alone. A child of California's term-limits movement, he is a political greenhorn, a nimble, scrappy, but untested lawmaker who won his first legislative election a mere 3 1/2 years ago.

Now, suddenly, Villaraigosa is one of the three mightiest men in state government. One minute, he's dueling with the governor on *The MacNeil/Lehrer News Hour*. The next, he's influencing how California spends its budget of $76 billion a year. Pundits predict that if he shines as speaker, he could become mayor of Los Angeles, his hometown.

An impetuous, charming, and unusually frank politician, Villaraigosa came from nothing and is now definitely something. A former student rebel, union organizer, and lifelong outsider, he is today very much on the inside, a genuine Establishment guy. His enormous Capitol office brims with antiques. A state driver takes him wherever he wants to go. Society's most powerful players—from Vice President Al Gore to bank presidents and titans of the entertainment world—are clamoring for two minutes of his time.

5. The writer answers the question she has all but asked by virtue of her structure:

All this begs the question: Is Antonio Villaraigosa—age 45, the first speaker from Los Angeles in a quarter-century—prepared for the job? Most politicians would toss back an unequivocal yes, emphasizing their tactical brilliance, perhaps, or their leadership prowess. Others would obfuscate, veer down a side stream into less perilous waters. Not Villaraigosa. Call it a deft use of candor, call it rookie recklessness, but he handles the query this way:

"Am I prepared? Absolutely not," he says without pause. "But we live in the era of term limits, where all of us are amateurs. The fact is, I got the job. And in the land of the blind, the one-eyed man is king."

6. The writer audaciously defines the protagonist's character (three paragraphs):

There are some things you should know about Antonio Villaraigosa. He was kicked out of one high school and dropped out of another. His arms bore tattoos—"Born to Raise Hell," "Tony Loves Arlene"—until his young son showed an alarming interest in the marks, and Villaraigosa paid doctors thousands of dollars to laser them off. He was tried for—and acquitted of—assault after a 1977 fight in an L.A. restaurant. He earned a law degree but failed to pass the state bar exam despite four tries. He fathered two children with two girlfriends before he was 25, and he drank, inhaled, and admits to other sins most politicians are too chicken to confess.

There are some other things you should know about Antonio Villaraigosa. His friends would run barefoot over broken glass for him, as he would for them. He is godfather to ten children. He outworks nearly everyone in a profession where workaholics abound. He is a hugger with a halogen smile and a habit of grasping your hand in both of his.

Oh, and another thing: Antonio Ramon Villaraigosa grew up so poor that he put strips of cardboard in his shoes when the soles wore out.

7. Now, having looped the essence of the story and the man, the writer is ready to take us to another scene, which she does by paralleling the structure of the opening anecdote:

The speaker is angry, positively steamed. It is a bright spring morning and the Assembly is at full boil, brawling over 1,309 bills. The phone rings, and an aide reports that crucial legislation to reform bilingual education is failing in committee. "Jesus Christ!" Villaraigosa roars. "Are these people stupid?" . . .

There is nothing emotional about the language—nothing. It is straightforward and sparse. But the structure drips with emotion: the sentences are generally short and punchy, full of movement, authority, and strong, well-reported examples, a tribute to showing rather than just telling, to putting the reader in the character's shoes. The writer has decided who Villaraigosa is, not merely as a politician but as a human being. She is courageous enough to have picked the scenes and defining characteristics rather than trotting out another party to offer a descriptive quote. She is the narrator, she is in control, and the reader will follow her anywhere because—not through emotional language but through emotional technique—she is connecting the reader to the character. She has found a way to first translate and then share those nonverbal impulses—the emotional truth—that she experienced while reporting the story. Her structure doesn't feel like an artifice, a tree on which to hang a bunch of facts, the way many features feel. It feels like the truth.

Just a Paragraph

Sometimes, in a shorter news feature, one paragraph gives that sense of real emotional connectedness to the reader. Nine paragraphs into a New York Times *first-anniversary story on the Oklahoma City federal building bombing, reporter Rick Bragg injected this perspective about the relatives of the victims:*

They have been asked to share their deepest feelings so many times by reporters and other total strangers that some of them answer with perfect television sound bites, or with long, eloquent passages that answer the most personal questions even before the reporters can ask them. There is nothing false in it; underlying the words is deep pain punctuated with tears. It is only that they are veterans at expressing their grief, anger and hatred. They are good at it.

That perspective is far more likely to be overheard from a reporter in a bar, talking to colleagues, than to make its way into a newspaper. But it takes more than guts to do this. It takes a subsequent paragraph that validates the proclamation, and in this case the writer had one.

"A year ago this week, Satan drove up Fifth Street in a Ryder truck," said Jannie Coverdale, whose two grandsons, Aaron, 5, and Elijah, 2, died in the blast along with 19 other children. "He blew my babies up. He may have looked like a normal man, but he was Satan. And I have to wonder, 'Where was God at 9:02 a.m. on April 19?'"

Sometimes the emotion is conveyed by an additional paragraph atop a story. Read the second paragraph of this L.A. Times *story first:*

Las Vegas is thinking the unthinkable: reining in those "one-armed bandits" and video gaming machines that have become such a ubiquitous force in the city of jackpots and hard luck.

Serviceable as a lead, right? But here's the first graph (making use of a rhetorical question, a technique that throws the story into a conversational mode), which showed the issue in a broader light:

LAS VEGAS—What's next? Banning booze on Bourbon Street? Tossing the bulls off the streets of Pamplona? Or, God forbid, removing roller-bladers from Venice Beach?

Las Vegas is thinking the unthinkable . . .

How Structure and Technique Complement Each Other

The writer has an anecdote. But a hoary old anecdote by itself does not guarantee grabbing the reader. Structure only gets you so far. The idea is to make the reader experience it—to put her, as we said earlier, in the shoes of the character. That's where technique comes in. In this case the USA Today *writer chose a two-pronged technique: the notion of the unknown, multiplied by repeating the same device several times. (Preachers have long understood the blessing of the latter trick.):*

FAIR LAWN, N.J.—Sheryl Lauchheimer didn't know that the crowded, battered old car in her rear-view mirror was one of the most notorious vehicles in the state.

She didn't know that in a matter of months, the red '77 Ford LTD would be involved in nine accidents.

Or that its owner would be involved in 13. Or that its driver would be involved in seven, including two that day.

She didn't know that the largest auto fraud ring in American history had come to this placid suburb, was rolling right up behind her as she waited at a stop sign.

Bang! In a second, Lauchheimer's Toyota was sliding into the intersection, into the path of a Volvo. Neighbors heard squealing tires, breaking glass, and crunching metal.

Lauchheimer leaped from the car scared but unhurt, unaware she had been deliberately rear-ended, that this accident was no accident at all.

Law enforcers say it's a scary and increasingly common insurance scam: Fill a junky car with passengers and collide with an unsuspecting (and fully insured) driver. Then claim injury and collect from the insurance companies.

The scheme, insurers say, has spread from the freeways of Southern California across the nation, to . . .

You can argue that the anecdote took a little too long to roll into the story, but the writer seemed to be anticipating that problem by foreshadowing in the fourth paragraph, alluding to "the largest auto fraud ring in American history. . . ." That bought him time. Besides, once he put you in that car, he had you. You were along for the ride. Oh, one more thing: Notice what wasn't in that story (and wouldn't appear until the eleventh graph): Our old friend, Mister Quote, the device we all got brainwashed into thinking has to be in a story by the fourth or fifth graph. Did you miss it? Me neither. The lesson: When your structure and technique can fuel the emotional drive of a story more effectively than a character's language, keep telling the story and don't look back.

The Drawback Is, This Is a Lot of Work

At a minimum, you should try to add 15 minutes to your writing time on shorter stories, stolen from some other part of your day, to put your notes aside after you have digested them, and ask yourself: Why does this story matter? What am I trying to say? What sequence of paragraphs will not only tell the story, but engage the reader with the nonverbal essence I felt out there in the street? Take fifteen minutes to lock yourself into a trance in search of the perspective, the transcendence, the emotional truth of the story.

A couple years ago, Barry Siegel spun a long detective yarn: A top medical sleuth, one of the country's premier experts in tracking and controlling infectious disease, was suddenly confronted with a rare potential outbreak of meningitis in the town of Mankato, Minn. After setting up the facts of the outbreak, and structuring it around his protagonist, Barry constructed these paragraphs that foreshadowed the main conflict of the story and summarized the emotional crucible we were about to enter:

. . . What he had, in fact, was an outbreak unprecedented in all the scientific literature. Before it ended six weeks later, the

"Neisseria meningitidis" bacteria would behave in Mankato in ways never before reported. In turn, the Minnesota health department and the Mankato community would wage a battle never before attempted. There would be moments of panic, accomplishment, and tragedy. Most of all, there would be uncertainty. When the bacteria's seige finally abated in mid-March, it would remain unclear just who had won.

Armed with state-of-the art tools, guided by years of experience, the experts could study, poke, and assault the bug, but they could not explain or master it. Forced to navigate uncharted waters, they could not know whether they were choosing the right course. In the end, they could not even say for sure whether they'd had any impact at all. . . .

Clearly, Barry put in more than 15 extra minutes, but his explanation of how he distilled his reported facts in search of the emotional truth—in this case, a dramatic narrative that chronicled the search for a cure—is instructive. Here are excerpts from an essay he wrote about the story:

For me, the first key to successful organization and writing is in the reporting. As I ride airplanes and conduct interviews, I try always to keep in mind what I will be doing when I get back to my desk, and what I will need. What I will need are characters, points of view, scenes, a conflict, a story line, and—above all—details. When I interview, I keep asking people to walk me through their experience minute by minute. I try to get them to recollect particulars, to not talk abstractly, to not talk in cliches.

. . . Flying home, running through everything in my mind, it all usually feels compelling. Then I sit down at my desk and find myself staring at a three-foot-high pile of interview notes, clips, articles, and briefs. Suddenly my compelling story looks like—well, a three-foot-high pile of notes. Boring, chaotic notes with no meaning or shape. Sitting down at my desk after returning from a reporting trip is for me always a daunting experience.

So the first thing I try to do is distill that three-foot-high pile into its essence.

. . . I typed my notes. Then I typed several types of "indexes" or summary distillations of my notes. At this point I'm trying to boil everything down so I can get my mind around the story.

. . . Chronology, characters, points of view, issues. Those are the elements in my raw material that I want to identify and isolate.

. . . When I was done typing up indexes and summaries, I had reduced the boring chaotic three-foot pile of notes into a few sheets of paper.

Then I just sat with those few sheets of paper before me, and tried to imagine my story. No computer, no pad of paper, no pen; just thinking at this stage. What I tried to imagine was not a research project or a newspaper article, but rather, a nonfiction short story. A nonfiction short story with character, point of view, plot, conflict.

. . . I reread the few pages, shuffled them, reread them, thought. Eventually, I began to feel I was mastering all the information I had, that I was getting my mind around the pile of notes. When I could scroll through all the events and details in my mind, without consulting my notes, I was ready to sketch out an outline.

Only now did I pick up a pen. I'd deconstructed, now I would reconstruct.

My favorite phrase in Barry's essay? ". . . so I can get my mind around the story."
It took Barry days to get there. He was swamped with a story of incredible complexity. Most of us are not afforded (or have yet to earn) this kind of expansive pursuit of a story. But we all have the same basic challenge—and we can all steal an extra 15 minutes per story to attempt to master the information, to get our minds around the story, to take that extra step in which the qualities of explanation and perspective can lift the ordinary story up a notch.

You Have to Take Chances

A young member of our staff was writing a standard daily about the random killing of a nine-year-old girl. His challenge, implicitly, was: There are so damn many of these tragedies, what technique could get the reader to care about this one? So he sacrificed the standard who-got-shot-this-time with a detailed description of the sheer randomness:

Drinking beers and joking in the bleary hours of the morning, the group of men playing cards in the courtyard of a Willowbrook apartment complex said they didn't think much of the confrontation when it happened.

Their neighbor, Sergio Chavez, had opened the screen door of his tiny clapboard cottage and brusquely told them to keep the noise down while his family struggled to sleep in the stifling heat.

But when Chavez slammed the door and climbed back into bed, one of the card-players got up from the game and stormed off to his truck.

Moments later, according to Jesus Alvarado, the man came back in a rage, yelling and swinging a pistol in the darkness. With his arm swaying haphazardly, he aimed at the screen door and opened fire.

After several shots, he stopped and ran away, leaving only the piercing sounds of a desperate father and a little girl crying in the balmy air.

"He shot my daughter! He shot my daughter!" rang out through the community of Mexican immigrants, a tight-knit group who often go surf-fishing together on the weekends. "He hit my family," Chavez cried.

His two young daughters, both sleeping on a piece of foam on the floor, were hit—7-year-old Janet in the neck, 9-year-old Crystal in the heart.

While Janet was listed in stable condition at a hospital Saturday afternoon, Crystal was dead before the ambulance arrived, family members said.

It takes eight paragraphs to find out that a nine-year-old girl died. But consider the tradeoff: The writer puts you in the house. He makes you understand, the way few daily crime stories do, how these insane shootings happen. Besides, by the fifth paragraph you are aware a child has been shot. The writer took you along for the emotional ride and made the story pay off before you lost interest.

Chapter 8: Creativity

I Want My Writing to Be More Sophisticated

Well, me too. Who hasn't looked in the mirror and wished he or she was saying more in his stories? Who hasn't wanted to write with a more interesting voice?

Consider a dozen or so qualities that contribute to sophisticated writing. To illustrate them, I pulled excerpts of Times *stories, all but one of which appeared in March or April of 2000. They're presented in an attempt to show the moment in a story when the piece rises from functional to meaningful, when it connects with the reader on a higher, more complex, more rewarding level.*

This is more than just writing. In each excerpt, the writer made good, hard choices in reporting—the extra trip to observe, the extra phone call to ask for perspective, the extra clips read to distill contextual wisdom.

Make yourself a promise: In the next story you write, try to inject at least two of the following sensibilities. The story after that, try to use at least three, and so on. No story allows for these qualities to be injected simultaneously or to the same degree, but we need more stories that use more of them more often. There are countless additional sensibilities. Look for them—study them—whenever you read.

Be Direct

1. Use the second person singular. We overdo this in everyday features, but it's a good technique (underlined below) if you need to create a feeling of immediacy in order to sell a complex notion:

> BANGALORE, INDIA—The latest wave reshaping the global economy springs not from Silicon Valley, nor from the canyons of Manhattan, but from offices and warehouses here.
>
> Visit <u>your doctor</u> and there's a chance <u>your file</u>, dictated over the phone, will be typed up in India and shot back overnight into the physician's computer.
>
> Miss the monthly payment on <u>your new refrigerator,</u> and the person who <u>calls to bug you</u> may be sitting in an office in New Delhi, 8,000 miles away.
>
> Request a different flight, and <u>your plane ticket</u>, scanned into a computer, may flash on a screen in Bombay, where a young college grad will punch in the change.
>
> As technology obliterates distance in the global marketplace, this impoverished country seems paradoxically poised to seize the latest opportunity like no other. Full of English-speaking university graduates desperate for work, India is rapidly becoming a magnet for service jobs ranging from the mundane to the cutting-edge.

2. When you're writing about something with a deeply shared context, like a block-buster movie, jump into it. By the second graph, the writer is already full of the character's defiance (underlined):

> With her skimpy skirts, bulging bustiers, and "cha-cha" heels, real-life toxic avenger Erin Brockovich is challenging conventional wisdom that dressing for success means wearing a power suit. Her signature sexy style, which she adopted as a teenager, has been both a tool and obstacle in her work as a researcher investigating ground-water contamination with attorney Ed Masry.
>
> She is judged by movie critics—and in real life—by how she dresses. <u>But would Brockovich ever dream of changing? Hell no</u>. She is a woman of substance who always seems to be overshadowed by her love of short skirts. But now she's a poster girl for those who are tired of being dismissed as bimbos. Her personal style has clearly become her professional style, and she flaunts it.
>
> "Certain days I'll come into work and Ed says, 'Brockovich has her war paint on,' because of the way I'm dressed," says the 39-year-old bombshell, who is played by Julia Roberts in the film that grossed just over $28 million on its opening weekend. "On days like that, I generally know there's going to be someone in my life, either from another law firm or on a case—usually a man—and I think it may give me an edge."

3. Talk about arcane subjects (such as university financing) with unvarnished terminology and simple conceptual truth (underlined):

> NEW YORK—Strip away tradition, ivy-covered walls, fancy laboratories, gray-muzzled scholars and <u>what's left at the foundation of all great universities is the same thing: money</u>.
>
> <u>That's the stuff</u> that made Harvard, Yale, and Princeton great over the past couple of hundred years. It's what Stanford spent lavishly in the '60s to build a world-class faculty and its reputation.
>
> And <u>it is the stuff</u> that in a relatively short time has transformed New York University from a mediocre commuter school into one of the nation's premier private universities—one with enough allure to attract thousands of students from California each year.
>
> NYU's make-over is emblematic of a resurging interest in urban education nationwide that has come with falling crime rates and a shift in what students want out of college.

4. Be audacious in profiling: Know enough about your subject to speak through her mind, as in this piece about a fallen Vietnamese aristocrat who made it rich in America as a restaurateur (underlined):

> . . . It isn't difficult to imagine her as a girl who was taught social skills, including how to address the help. The picture that's harder to conceive is of Elizabeth, then known as Ngoc, as a gawky teenager in San Francisco, who was teased for having a funny accent, a weird name and the wrong clothes. It's doubtful she would be here now, presiding over the elegant party that happens nightly at the corner of Bedford Drive and Little Santa Monica Boulevard, if fate hadn't messed with the good life she knew in Vietnam.
>
> Remember the moment midway through *Gone With the Wind* when a ragged Scarlett O'Hara, silhouetted against a fiery orange sky, swears, "As God is my witness, I'll never be hungry again"? Elizabeth and her sister Hannah could play that scene perfectly and mean every word. Except in their case, the oath would be, "You'll never look down on my family again." Like Scarlett, they saw a society crushed, then used intelligence, determination and charm to fulfill private promises made when times were hard.

5. When you've got news, proclaim it:

> SAN FRANCISCO—The wild dot-com party is ending for some companies. And as the hangovers take hold among Internet stocks, many of the Web's retailers and information services may soon become dot-gones.
>
> In the last few days auditors for several well-known Web businesses issued warnings that the companies' survival is in "substantial doubt." On Thursday, drkoop. com, a leading health-information site, and Value America, a PC retailer, received such warnings, sending their share prices near all-time lows. A day earlier, CDNow, a top online music seller and one of the most popular sites on the Web, saw its share price plummet on news of a severe cash crunch.
>
> And Peapod. com, an online grocery service, said it is urgently seeking a buyer before its dwindling cash reserves run out.

Add Historical Perspective

. . . as in a middle segment of this news analysis about the LAPD Ramparts Division scandal and the unwillingness of the LAPD to cooperate with the D.A.:

The explosive conflict between the chief and district attorney occurs against two backdrops, one historically rich, the other politically hot.

For years, police and prosecutors have battled over one thing or another, from the Police Department's resistance to allowing prosecutors to wade too deeply into the scenes of police shootings to the testy disagreements about which agency was most responsible for blowing the case against O. J. Simpson. In some cases, those disputes have grown personal. Garcetti and his deputies feuded with then-Chief Daryl F. Gates over prosecutors' rights to inspect crime scenes and interview witnesses to police shootings.

Those disagreements continued through the 1980s and 1990s, by which time Garcetti had been elected district attorney, and Police Chief Willie L. Williams was at the helm of the LAPD.

For the most part, however, those spats have been run-of-the-mill flare-ups between police and prosecutors, higher profile than in most cities but otherwise not that unusual.

This one is much bigger than a spat. Parks repeatedly has said Garcetti was going too slow in his Rampart investigation, refusing to prosecute the Rampart officers accused of wrongdoing. Garcetti has insisted that he wants to go further and deeper, gathering evidence for major felony prosecutions in Rampart and, if necessary, in other police divisions.

That has made the latest confrontation something else altogether . . .

Use a Question as a Focusing Device
Watch the relationship (underlined) between this interior graph and the question that follows:

So far, newspaper companies are holding their own against Internet sites in the battle for classified advertising, source of 45 percent of the revenue of large papers. Technology research institutes predict that newspapers will lose 18 percent of their classified revenues in the next four years.

Why then is *Tribune,* one of the most profitable newspaper companies in the country, making this bid? Because it wants to expand its efforts on the Internet and prove those predictions wrong. *Tribune* believes that the mass media's ability to attract and deliver customers to advertisers "are undervalued today," said Jack Fuller, head of *Tribune*'s publishing division. . . .

Use Your Own Voice Instead of Quotes
Report the story hard enough to develop a voice of authority that lets you push quotes out of the way for at least six or seven graphs to let the story fully develop:

> The class sweetheart is Fatima Anda, always smiling, always sitting in front. Her baby son is named for a childhood friend, recently murdered.
>
> Seated behind her is Diana Acosta, who had been to the funerals of four friends by the time she was 18. Nearby is Jesse Salcido, whose childhood friends were all in gangs. And there is Rachel Goytia, who thinks her father may have been the victim of a gang murder when she was 6, but she isn't sure, because no one will give her a straight story.
>
> They are classmates at East Los Angeles College, and they share a goal: to work in law enforcement.
>
> It is a social phenomenon in tough Eastside neighborhoods. You see it in juvenile camps, high schools and colleges. I want to be a probation officer, they say, or, I want to be a cop. An East Los Angeles probation officer says half her offenders want to work in probation. At Bell High School, a counselor says law enforcement rivals teaching as the most popular career goal.
>
> Some make it; most don't. But the simple aspiration offers a glimpse of Los Angeles at its best and worst. Dreams of a life in law enforcement are a legacy of the violence that has touched the lives of a generation of young people who are now hungry for redemption.
>
> It's like a morality play—a kind of revenge of the decent: Certain kids may spend half their lives acting friendly with the gang members down the street, avoiding fights and biding their time. But they're coming back someday—as cops.
>
> Fatima Anda, 21, explained it this way: "You came from here. You were raised here. You have to do something for your little brothers, your nephews, your neighbors."
>
> Like the Irish and Italians before them, Anda and her classmates represent the talented offspring of urban working-class immigrants. . . .

Use Only Those Quotes That Matter
. . . as in this story, in which the writer kept re-interviewing her subjects, determined to get quotes (underlined) that could bring common-sense wisdom to the abstract.

PALO ALTO—It's happening again. Some physicists are claiming to have solved the greatest mystery in the universe.

They say they have found "dark matter"—impossibly elusive particles that make up nearly all of the universe, yet have never been captured, created in a lab, or even detected.

Previous claims have popped up regularly since the early 1980s. But as the charmingly named dark-matter candidates—neutrinos, monopoles, MACHOs, black holes, and dwarfs of various colors—fail to stand up to experimental and theoretical proofs, they fade faster than presidential campaign promises.

<u>"It's like Elvis. There are sightings every so often that are never confirmed,"</u> said Rocky Kolb, who heads the cosmology department at the Fermi National Accelerator Laboratory in Batavia, Ill.

. . . Even if the Italian-Chinese team has fallen short, the theoreticians believe somebody is on the verge of snaring their quarry—thanks to spectacular leaps in technology that can detect barely perceptible flickers of energy and motion.

<u>"We've ruled out a lot of suspects and now an arrest is imminent," said Mike Turner, an astrophysicist at the University of Chicago. "When you're working a big case</u>—think JonBenet Ramsey or O.J.—<u>you've got to check out every lead."</u>

These were the last two graphs:

It's also possible that dark matter could be made of something so strange that it hasn't yet been theorized, something so elusive that humans may never detect it.

<u>"There's no guarantee that it will be in a form that we can ever discover," said Kolb. "That's what wakes me up at night in a cold sweat."</u>

When You Work Hard Enough to Get Great Quotes, Have the Guts to Use a Lot of Them

. . . as in a section of this column that watched a march by striking janitors. Look how well the underlined language sets us up for the quotes that follow, and how each quote illustrates a specific desire—a technique that could be employed in many feature stories.

. . . Marches don't happen unless the people involved have begun to see themselves as players. <u>Unless someone has found the voice to ask: What do we want?</u>

"For my children to get ahead," said Rosalia Lopez. She marched, sweating, past a gleaming Chevy Suburban, hunter green, leather interior, parked curbside. "For them to maybe someday have"—she gestured—"one of those."

"Maybe one house, someday," shouted Carlos Santana, new father, over the ear-splitting chants of "Si! Se Puede!" "Maybe in Santa Monica."

"For each of my children to have their own rooms," dreamed Enrique Gaspar.

"To take my little girl to Knott's Berry Farm once a year," Karina Martinez replied.

"To send my son to university," said Daisy Herrera.

"To be able to afford a computer with a hookup to the Internet," said 17-year-old Manuel Rincon, marching at his father's side.

"To finish my education, because I am going to school, so I can work as electricity—I mean, work as an electrician," Max Salvador offered, his broad Oaxacan face concentrating hard on his second language. "And to own a house. Not a big house. But a house that is in a quiet place, like this place. And maybe"—now he was laughing out loud—"one Land Cruiser! Hey, who knows?". . .

When Writing a Review, Draw a Clear Line between the Work's Aspirations and Its Results

. . . as in the middle of this arts commentary on the Vietnam Veterans Memorial, in which the most important perception—"we needed a place to grieve"—was carefully set up:

. . . the Vietnam memorial is successful precisely because it's modern, not in spite of it. A traditional, representational statue in marble or bronze, complete with the standard classical repertoire, would have spelled disaster. There are two reasons, and they are intimately related.

First, a traditional memorial would have instantly historicized the Vietnam War. The bronze statues and classical motifs familiar to most war memorials would have anchored the event being commemorated firmly in the past. The soul- and body-shattering trauma of war often demands just this sort of public response. Imagery redolent of the past solemnly sanctifies the dead, who immediately join a collective pantheon of ancestral authority. And the living, faced with a familiar and comforting symbol of history, are reassured through an implicit declaration: "We have survived."

No event since the Civil War has had such a profound and wrenching effect on the national sense of self. America was literally torn in two, split into raw, polarized, and seemingly irreconcilable camps. The war had been over for just six years when the competition for the memorial's design concluded, and the wound in the American psyche remained fresh and deep. However much we wanted to put the awful episode behind us, there was important work left to do.

We needed a place to grieve. It had to be a public place, too, where the personal expression of loss could be shared. . . .

Connect the Macro and the Micro
1. The writer profiled a striking janitor in order to humanize the impact of economics:

By the time janitor Rosa Alvarenga left El Salvador nine years ago, forces were already in motion that would push her to a picket line in Woodland Hills.

High immigration from impoverished countries, weak unions and an economic downturn all combined to lower paychecks for a whole class of semiskilled workers. Now low wages for blue-collar jobs are a given in Los Angeles, even in a booming economy, even as workers like Alvarenga struggle to make ends meet.

What is perhaps more significant, outsourcing and corporate consolidation—two of the sweeping economic changes of our time—have obscured the chain of responsibility between those who directly benefit from manual labor, such as building tenants, and those who do the work, such as janitors.

Alvarenga's employer, OneSource, an Atlanta-based subsidiary of a company headquartered in Belize, is as anonymous to her as she is to the office workers whose toilets she cleans.

The effect is that both sides in the countywide janitors strike, which entered its fourth day Thursday and has become increasingly heated, are fighting a war with phantoms, loaded with symbolism and misunderstanding.

To Alvarenga, who cleans two floors of a gleaming high-rise, working alone from 6 p.m. to 2:30 a.m. . . .

2. The writer noticed that a planned major realignment of bus routes played havoc with a route traveled primarily by the working poor as they made their way to jobs in the homes of the affluent:

The sun is still sleeping as nannies, maids and hotel workers wait for the first Route 57 bus in downtown Santa Ana. The time is 4:57 a.m.

These Spanish-speaking immigrants are already commuting to jobs that begin at 7 or 8 in the morning on south Orange County's tony coastline.

The longest leg of the trip, to Newport Beach and beyond, is on the 57 bus, which traverses 16.6 miles of Orange County from northeast to southwest, from working class to upper class, from roofs of aging gray shingle to those of new Spanish tile.

The 57 bus has become a second home for a tight-knit immigrant community of thousands of riders. They spend about four hours a day traveling on it, transferring to it, or waiting for it. Now, a plan to end 57 bus service to Newport Center has them facing even longer commutes—an extra 22 minutes each way by one estimate—and in some cases, a third bus connection.

Transit planners say the change will straighten circuitous routes and make the system more efficient. The modifications will result in even less time with families for the riders on the 57, many of whom already work 10- to 12-hour days. Some worry that the commute time could threaten their jobs, or at best force them to pay higher bus fares.

To them, something less tangible is also at stake. Without the Newport Center as a transit hub, they will be robbed of the few short moments of camaraderie that break up long, numbing days of caring for other people's children, tending to lawns, and cleaning homes.

Every morning when they arrive in Newport Beach, halfway to their destination, 30 or so nannies and maids form a human circle just blocks from Fashion Island, one of California's poshest shopping centers. Waiting for connecting buses or rides from their employers for as long as an hour, they thrive on gossip, tacos, and sales pitches from one maid who doubles as an Avon lady. . . .

When You Engage in Wordplay, Connect Your Playfulness to the Organization of the Story

1. The surfing terminology (underlined) is sustained through the nut graph:

When it comes to riding killer waves, David Skelly totally rips. It's only when he surfs the paper swells of bureaucracy that he gets full-on thrashed.

Skelly, an Encinitas marine engineer, has designed what is expected to be the nation's first artificial surf reef: a 2,000-ton pile of sandbags to be submerged off the shores of El Segundo, near Los Angeles International Airport.

The proposed reef is intended to reverse the wave-flattening effects of a 17-year-old jetty there and transform Dockweiler State Beach into a surfing mecca, a place where overjoyed wave riders won't even notice the blast of jets overhead or the smell of the bordering Hyperion sewage plant.

Trouble is, members of the San Clemente-based Surfrider Foundation, which conceived the idea and hired Skelly for the job, figured the warehouse-sized reef would be finished four years ago. Instead, <u>they've found themselves caught in a protracted funding and environmental riptide.</u>

2. Here, the punchy lead graph leads to a newsy second graph, but returns to a playful tone in the third:

Memo to Disneyland cast members: Walt had one. Now you can too.

Walt Disney Co. said Monday it has scrapped a 43-year-old ban on mustaches for its theme park employees. The move is a minor concession for the Magic Kingdom, which continues to have one of the strictest grooming codes of any American employer.

Beards are still prohibited. Nose rings and purple hair? Forget it. And no Elvis look-alikes please: Sideburns below the bottom of the ears aren't allowed.

But in a letter going out this week to 12,000 workers at Disneyland and its four parks in Florida, Disney Attractions President Paul Pressler said the mustache edict was lifted because . . .

3. Parallelism works (underlined) when it's truly parallel:

He was a young engineer not long out of college and recently married. <u>His new job: Help build a nuclear reactor.</u>

Thirty-five years later, Jarlath Curran is nearing retirement age. <u>But he's got one more thing to do: Help tear down that reactor.</u>

Curran, 61, is one of the reasons Southern California Edison Co. decided to start decommission now of Unit I of the San

Onofre Nuclear Generating Station. The company wanted some of the engineers who built and ran it for years to help dismantle the 450-megawatt reactor before they retire.

Find an Emerging Trend on Your Beat
. . . as in this piece about how an increasing number of home sales were being affected by feng shui, a tale a real estate writer kept hearing from her sources. That was quantification enough (see underlined material):

> Nerissa Rosete fell in love with a pricey South Orange County home, especially its impressive view of the mountains. She entered escrow, putting $20,000 down.
>
> But she walked away from the deal, losing half her down payment, after a consultant noted the way the backyard steeply dropped off to meet Interstate 5. It was, he warned her, bad feng shui: The receding yard would prompt energy to rush out of the home.
>
> Once again, the 3,000-year-old Chinese practice of feng shui, which teaches manipulation of one's physical surroundings to bring about balance and success, had shaken up the real estate market.
>
> <u>Nearly every real estate office in Southern California seems to have a tale about how buyers or sellers, including a large proportion of non-Chinese, have made surprising compromises in pursuit of good feng shui.</u>
>
> One sign is the rapidly growing field of feng shui consulting. Other signals include transactions like Rosete's that are falling through when a consultant vetoes a home. Some deals are taking longer to close because of buyer demands for a feng shui inspection. Some feng shui consultants are issuing certificates that sellers can use to prove a home's worthiness.

Use Your Life—Even the Mundane Part—as a Source for Stories
. . . like the reporter who was so aggravated by the unreadable jury summons in his mailbox that he wrote a page one piece:

> The Los Angeles County court system has come up with a new jury summons form so dense that even some judges can't make sense of it.
>
> The form, resembling a cross between a mortgage application and a deli menu, has generated a flood of complaints—including one from a Pasadena resident called to jury duty: Judge Lance Ito. He filled it out incorrectly.

"Even the IRS couldn't dream up something so complicated!" Ito fumed. "Holy smokes, this is horrible."

The new form was drafted for the Los Angeles County courts' new jury system and is designed to streamline the process for the 4.5 million prospective jurors contacted yearly.

But as court officials and committees insisted that more and more information be included, the summons form that was once relatively easy to understand has become a complex, text-laden document with folding instructions that appear to require a knowledge of origami.

Create an Explanatory Tone

Here, in the middle of the story, the reporter distilled complex information into a chronological flow to show us how a coastal construction permit was muddled by power politics. Admire how the simple language and transitional structure (underlined) compensates for the complexity, and how those two colons in the fourth graph of the segment also make the ride easier:

. . . The conflict started conventionally enough. Trusts established by billionaire Eli Broad, television magnate Haim Saban, and Nancy Daly, Riordan's wife, picked up six Malibu parcels from Pepperdine University and set out to demolish the houses that stood on them and then to replace them with three larger homes.

Given the size and configuration of what they had in mind, that meant cutting off the view of the ocean from Pacific Coast Highway. <u>The Coastal Commission begged to differ</u>, and demanded that each of the three home sites—which average about 100 feet along the highway—include 20 feet of "view corridor."

<u>That didn't sit well with the trio</u>. Broad, for instance, envisioned a house designed by Pritzker Prize–winning architect Richard Meier, the man behind the Getty Museum, and understandably was not happy with the idea of his landmark home constrained by a corridor so that passing motorists could glance at the water as they shot by at 50 miles an hour.

<u>So Broad and his friends made the Coastal Commission an offer</u>: If the panel would let them cut off the ocean views around their homes, they would buy an 80-foot stretch of a nearby beach and protect it from development. <u>Their argument</u>: The Riordans, Sabans and Broads would get their houses, and the public would not only get more view—in many ways, a better view, since it would be in one chunk rather than three 20-foot intervals—but also public access to that beach.

That was all well and good for them, and it satisfied the Coastal Commission staff. <u>But for the neighbors who live near the beach</u>, it was no good at all. Why, they asked, should their beach be made more accessible to the public just so their famous and powerful would-be neighbors wouldn't have to put up with anyone looking over their shoulders at the sunset?

<u>And, this being Malibu</u>, the neighbors who complained— though not necessarily of the stature of a big-city mayor and a couple of business titans known for their political savvy and lavish contributions to candidates and causes—are no slouches.

In a Profile, Use Enough Detail to Let the Reader Truly Visualize Your Character
1. From a profile of a disabled rocker/surfer:

> . . . Days by the coast have left Tuduri perma-tanned. His hair is '70s long and feathered like David Cassidy's, only grayer now that he is 52. His voice is tinged by the drawl of rocker culture, but is disarmingly upbeat. There is no bravado from a man who knows he probably should be dead. He looks deep into your eyes when he speaks, peering over the top of red glasses balanced on the bridge of his nose and from beneath bushy gray eyebrows. His left thumb, which occasionally quakes, bears a red star, so worn by the chafing of a drumstick it looks like a prison tattoo. . . .

2. From the lead of a news feature about a battered woman who benefitted from donated plastic surgery:

> Hard as she tries, Tosha McClintock can't get used to her new face.
>
> Her chin, which had been beaten until it was barely visible, feels full and heavy now, the result of a reconstructive implant. Her ears, which resembled cauliflowers from repeated pummeling, feel small and flat against her head, sewn closed, no longer bulging with cartilage.
>
> And she can breathe out of her nose again. It had been flattened for so long—a favorite target of her ex-boyfriend's fists— that McClintock, 29, forgot what it was there for, what it had ever really looked like. She touches her new nose absently now, tracing over it, pushing on it. Sometimes she'll catch a glimpse of her profile when she turns to look at something, and she has to remind herself what it is.

Show Your Readers the Nuances of How the World Works
Check the language (underlined) in the sixth graph of a labor dispute story. It let you know that what you were watching was part stunt and part serious:

> More than 2,000 teachers gathered at Los Angeles Unified School District headquarters Tuesday to decry a labor contract proposal offered by interim Supt. Ramon C. Cortines that for the first time would link teachers' pay to performance.
>
> Chanting, "The district says take-backs, we say fight back!" teachers from schools as far away as San Pedro arrived downtown by the busload to oppose the proposal to rate their performance with test scores, as well as Cortines' plan to take away teachers' authority to elect coordinators and department chairmen. . . .
>
> . . . <u>On one level, the protests are typical of the maneuvering that often occurs early in labor talks. But the outpouring underscored the degree to which Cortines' proposals have struck at issues that are hot buttons for many union activists.</u>

Chapter 9: Schizophrenia in Editing

Getting Rid of Fat

Fat haunts too many of our stories. One more rewrite, one more pass of a writer's or editor's eye—one more courageous strike against flab—can restore the original sense of urgency and purpose that we too often lose in the drive to cram the proper facts and perspective into a piece.

Here we offer two remedies. First, some examples of purposefulness and, second, some specific suggestions on how to discipline your self-editing.

#1: Role-Playing
Do you conscientiously assign each paragraph a distinct role? Look how clearly each of the first six graphs in this example carry out a specific task. If you can't find the same graph-by-graph tracking in your copy, it's a tip something's wrong.

Graph 1: Context/set-up
Few people in Hollywood have the ability to say yes. The power to green light a motion picture—to commit the resources to make it—rests with a handful of studio executives whose names are well known throughout the industry.

Graph 2: Introduce character function
A. Fredric Leopold is not one of those names. But the 78-year-old lawyer's stamp of approval matters as much as any mogul's. Leopold is dean of the script vetters. He dissects would-be movies and television shows for a living, looking for vulnerabilities: libelous depictions, trademark or copyright infringement, violations of privacy.

Graph 3: Show significance of function
If Leopold finds none, he will "clear" a script, an endorsement required by insurance companies before they will underwrite a project. But if the soft-spoken grandfather deems a project too risky, chances are it won't get made.

Graph 4: Expand on significance of function
"No one in their right mind will commence principal photography on a project unless they've got approval from an insurance carrier," said Doug Mirell, a lawyer with the Los Angeles firm Loeb & Loeb. "And they're not going to get that unless they've got a clean bill of health from somebody like Fred."

*Graph 5: Deeper explanation of function to prepare reader
for example*

Leopold and other clearance experts are the actuaries of the entertainment industry. Often working with professional researchers, these lawyers seek to calculate—and, ideally, remove—all risks of potential legal action. They know that, in the best case, a lawsuit will run up sizable legal fees. At worst, it can halt a film's distribution.

Graph 6: The example

Consider the case of *Lebbeus Woods vs. Universal Studios,* in which Woods, an artist, alleged that the 1995 movie *12 Monkeys* had copied his drawing of a wall-mounted chair. . . .

The harder you work on disciplining your sequence, the more likely you'll be to develop an instinctive "feel" that makes sure each graph has its own job, and does it.

#2: Be Tougher on Yourself about Getting to the Point

Sometimes you can give each paragraph a specific role to play, yet be sabotaged by leisure. Consider the following front-page story from the New York Times:

On Aug. 18, 1587, on a coastal island called Roanoke in what is now North Carolina, a couple named Ananias and Eleanor Dare produced a daughter and named her Virginia, in honor of both the colony where they lived and of Elizabeth I, known as England's virgin queen. The baby, as schoolbooks have long noted, was the first English child born in America.

Four days later, the colony's leader sailed for home to obtain supplies. But England was preparing to meet the Spanish Armada and no ships could be spared for the New World. Three years passed before a relief expedition returned to Roanoke Island. It found no one. Virginia Dare and all the other colonists had vanished.

Ever since, the fate of the Lost Colony of Roanoke has presented one of the most baffling and enduring mysteries in American history.

Now at least part of an answer, and possibly the key to the mystery, has emerged from centuries-old cypress trees in southeastern Virginia and northeastern North Carolina, not far from Roanoke Island. Analysis of the annual growth rings of the trees has shown that in a colossal piece of misfortune, the Roanoke colonists—and the Jamestown settlers who followed them a few years later—arrived in the worst droughts of the last 800 years in that part of the country.

"If it weren't for bad luck, these English wouldn't have had any luck at all," said Dennis Blanton, an archeologist at the College of William and . . .

Interesting? Yep. Acceptable? Nope. What mythical reader has time to plod through it, what with six or seven other stories on the same front page? Was there news here? Yep. It was a newly released study. Did the writer feel like doing the hard work of distillation for the reader—sacrificing those two tortured set-up graphs and the quote in favor of first explaining what the facts meant? Nope. Consider (ahem) what the L.A. Times' *same-day story said:*

> The worst droughts of the past 800 years probably were responsible for wiping out the first British settlers who tried to colonize North America, according to researchers who have reconstructed the weather of the era when European colonists struggled for a toehold in the New World.
>
> "If the English had tried to find a worse time to launch their settlements in the New World, they could not have done so," said Dennis B. Blanton, director of the William and Mary Center for Archeological Research.
>
> Severe drought may have doomed Britain's first settlement, known to history as the "Lost Colony" of Roanoke Island, N.C., the researchers report. And, but for a timely and prolonged rainy season in 1612 that ended an unusually severe seven-year drought, the second attempt, at Jamestown, Va., might have succumbed as well.
>
> At the height of the epic Jamestown drought, the "starving time," as the colonists called it, "these folks literally packed their bags and were prepared to call it quits," Blanton said.
>
> The new research, published today in the journal *Science,* is helping historians gain a growing appreciation for how even the fate of nations can turn on the whims of weather. It comes at a time when scientists are increasingly voicing concern. . . .

Something else that often keeps us from getting to the point is the extra, flabby step in the dance from the anecdote to the nut—the material we like, and refuse to take out even though it has a deadening effect on the pace of the lead. Think about what you'd cut from this New York Times *example:*

> WINSTON-SALEM, N.C.—Seven years ago, George Howard's telephone began to ring repeatedly with anonymous, belligerent calls. Wherever he went in Winston-Salem—to church, to the supermarket—the snide comments seemed to follow.

It was not that Dr. Howard, an epidemiologist at the Wake Forest University School of Medicine, had been charged with child molestation, or that he was trying to bring a toxic waste dump to town. Rather, he had just published research concluding that cigarette smoking and exposure to secondhand smoke could hasten hardening of the arteries. He had done so while living and working in the hometown of the R. J. Reynolds Tobacco Company, a city that clings defiantly to its bumper-sticker creed: "Thank you for smoking."

"There was a lot of pressure," Dr. Howard said, "a lot of negative feedback, a lot of harassment. People called me and fussed at me, said I was not loyal and this, that, and the other. I was a little bit worried. I wasn't moving my family out of the house or anything, but it made me think."

Earlier this year, Dr. Howard published another study, this one concluding that 30,000 to 60,000 deaths a year nationwide can be attributed to secondhand smoke. This time, his phone has been silent. Of the comments he has heard from acquaintances at church and the supermarket, 98 percent, he estimates, have been supportive.

"I think," he said, "that there's been a dramatic change in this city."

Just as there has been a profound shift in the politics of tobacco in Washington, so has there been a marked change in the civic culture of Winston-Salem, a city identified more than any other with the American tobacco industry.

Not so long ago . . .

The fat the writer should have removed is in the second and third paragraphs. They're what blocks a smooth path from the protagonist's first experience to his second—the contrast that symbolizes the change in Winston-Salem.

This is a classic problem—the writer embellishes a device, rather than stripping down the device so it can perform its true function: leading us to the promised land. In this case, the writer just as easily could have said (in 101 fewer words, or 41 percent less space):

WINSTON-SALEM, N.C.—Seven years ago, George Howard's telephone began to ring repeatedly with anonymous, belligerent calls.

Dr. Howard, an epidemiologist at the Wake Forest University School of Medicine, had just published research concluding that cigarette smoking and exposure to secondhand smoke could hasten hardening of the arteries. He had done so while living and working in the hometown of the R. J. Reynolds Tobacco Company, a city that clings defiantly to its bumper-sticker creed: "Thank you for smoking."

Earlier this year, Dr. Howard published another study, this one concluding that 30,000 to 60,000 deaths a year nationwide can be attributed to secondhand smoke. This time, his phone has been silent. Of the comments he has heard from acquaintances at church and the supermarket, 98 percent, he estimates, have been supportive.

"I think," he said, "that there's been a dramatic change in this city."

Ruthlessness in Self-Editing

Okay, writers, here's the naked truth: Your space is being cut. The 50-inch profile you wanted to do is going to become a 40-inch profile, maybe even a 35-inch profile. The 22-inch daily you had your heart set on is going to be 18. But within that pain is a discovery: There's some value in being forced to write shorter. It makes you take a harder look at the self-indulgent tendencies all of us bring to our writing. It makes you spend more time on self-editing, which almost all of us need to improve. And it helps you bring more focus to your piece.

Jill Leovy gave us an example the other day with a taut profile of a former homeless man who was graduating from USC and headed toward a master's degree. I was first attracted by how much of Jill's own voice was in the piece, how much better it worked than a story that relied on quotes, how stripped-down it felt, how fast it read. Consider the top (with those few quotes in boldface):

It's just over two miles from skid row to USC. It took Daniel Rodriguez a decade to complete the journey.

An odyssey that began in a skid row mission has ended, for now, at a USC graduation ceremony, where the 43-year-old Rodriguez, a high school dropout and former penniless street fighter, received a bachelor's degree in history with honors.

Next will come a master's degree—he has been accepted to graduate school at USC—and then a law degree. He promises.

But no achievement is likely to mean as much as this one.

Wearing a cap and gown Thursday marked the fulfillment of a goal Rodriguez has pursued with the intensity of a man obsessed.

It took nerve, talent, and monk-like austerity to make this climb that led from the public library to Los Angeles Trade Tech to USC. That, and many helping hands along the way.

"The miracle," is what he calls his nine-year quest for an education. **"God has been so good to me."**

In the two years he has been at USC, Rodriguez has earned a 3.5 grade-point average. He won scholarships to pay for his education, and he has landed two other awards for service and scholarship.

Even as Rodriguez collected accolades, he let few people know of his past, not even his senior thesis advisor, history professor and State Librarian Kevin Starr. Few knew he had been homeless, that he was still living on skid row when he started at USC.

There is nothing in Rodriguez's appearance today to suggest his years on the margins. He is slight and extremely youthful-looking. He has an amiable, intelligent air, and wins friends easily. At Los Angeles Trade Tech, the community college he attended while on skid row, he was elected student body president.

But at USC, he is distinguished by a kind of separateness, and an all-consuming commitment to his studies.

USC is no longer as white as it once was. One in six students today is Latino. But Rodriguez feels ill at ease among younger, whiter, richer students—hordes of them hanging out in Bermuda shorts and bikinis, blasting stereos on fraternity lawns near his home.

He beams intensity from every pore. Always in a hurry, and completely overloaded, it is as if he needs to remain in constant motion to sustain his trajectory.

"I don't have a social life," he said with particular emphasis, implying that it's not just a byproduct of his schedule; it's a principle.

His small, furnished room near the campus is nearly bare except for books. In a closet are his notebooks from all his years of college and university—eight total, six of them at Trade Tech.

Those early notebooks from his Trade Tech classes are yellowed now. Their content seems almost fantastically low-level: There are pages full of simple arithmetic, past and present perfect verb tenses: "Mike saw the bus. Mike has seen the bus."

On top of these is a recent USC paper on the Byzantine Empire in the twelfth century. It is written crisply, academically, the prose of an advanced history student at a top university.

It seems impossible that the same person could have done both it and the notebooks. **"Looking at them, sometimes I want to cry,"** he said.

The apartment also contains photos of his graduations and one of his adult daughter, from a relationship long ago, and a 5-year-old grandson.

Rodriguez admits that his daughter grew up without him. **"But she has forgiven me,"** he said.

There is a faded photo of his grandmother in the Dominican Republic. She is sitting on the grass, perhaps at a picnic, gazing unsmilingly into the camera. Rodriguez contemplates it with affection: **"That's what you call tough love,"** he said.

There is one more photo: It's of him as a young child at his first Communion in the Dominican Republic. In it, he stands ramrod straight in a white shirt. Something in it recalls the man today, not the one in those many grim years in between. **"This is me,"** he said. The skid row years **"were not me."**

In the Dominican Republic, Rodriguez had excelled in Catholic school. After immigrating with his family at the age of 15 to New York's Washington Heights neighborhood, he excelled in fighting.

"We went to school to fight," he said. **"We didn't go there to learn."**

That's 53 words of quotes in the first 759 words of the story, or about seven percent of the story. You or I would kill for that level of body fat at our annual physical, and you and I should aspire to inject the same kind of leanness in our writing. But eschewing quotes is only part of it. Here's Jill's description of how a harsh eye toward your own work—the glory of those "miserable cuts"—pays off:

I like the 45-inch story. It's completely maddening, but it seems to make my writing stronger and it's taught me to be ruthless.

For me, those stories are all about cutting. It's like a game. Length is the adversary, 45 inches the goal. Turn it in at 45, and you win.

I'm greedy, so I start by assuming it's Christmas and I can have everything. I spin this sprawling 80-inch monster with my whole notebook in it—all my best stuff.

Then comes the miserable cuts.

For what it's worth, here are my personal brevity rules:

First, the best newspaper feature stories have only one idea, beaten like a dead horse. State the one idea in the lead, write every graph about the one idea, end the story with the one idea. This really helps in cutting.

In the Skid Row story, the one idea is that this down-and-out guy became successful. So, presto! Everything that doesn't pertain to that gets tossed.

After that, omission is defeat. If something really belongs, I dock myself a point if I cut it just to save space. Better to keep it, but in a stripped-down form without details, examples, or quotes. You usually need only one sentence to make sure an idea is represented. Out with the ten graphs on various people who helped Mr. Skid Row! Just say he got a lot of help. The reward for being short is that you get to be dense.

There's also the usual stuff: Cut something you love. Cut all adverbs. Cut adjectives, especially those that aren't about concrete visual facts—blue is OK; proud, less so.

Last, sketch, don't paint. In features, you stop the narration at regular points to insert a moment in which time stops and the reader sees a picture. This is great, but it takes up space, so you have to let a lot of good detail go.

There's a line from an Archibald MacLeish poem: "For all the history of grief, an empty doorway and a maple leaf." It's about poetry. But see how vivid it is? The point is, two good details are usually enough. Often, one is.

Chapter 10: "Coping with Pressure"

Ten Things Reporters Want from Their Editors . . .

1. I want you to listen to me. I want your full, undivided attention. I don't want you staring at your screen, or answering computer messages, or taking phone calls when we're talking about a story.
2. I want to be able to brainstorm with you. To bounce ideas off you without feeling that you automatically have to pass judgment. I want you to contribute, not dominate.
3. I want you to respect my syntax. I want to feel as though as long as I'm writing clearly and purposefully, the choice of words is up to me. I want to sound like me, not you.
4. I want you to help me improve the integrity of my story. Concentrate on structure, not picky copy editing. Tell me what ideas or images don't work or can be improved. Develop a structural vocabulary that can articulate this. Help me bring more context, wisdom, and perspective to my work.
5. Don't rewrite me unless you have to. If we're not on deadline, tell me what you want me to do differently, send the story back to me, and let me try to do it myself.
6. As the reporting process unfolds, let me discover the story. Hold back on prejudging it, or dictating how I should pursue it. Let me explore the landscape and learn from it.
7. Tell me the truth. If a story has been targeted for a certain placement, length, or tone by your bosses, tell me what politics are involved, what battles we'll have to fight, why the story is holding, or why it needs to be cut. Let me participate in the idiocy that sometimes colors our business.
8. Play the role of a reader for me. Make fewer pronouncements and ask more questions—questions that demonstrate your interest and help me understand how certain sentences or combinations trigger certain questions in a reader's mind.
9. Balance the way I'm used. Remember the proportion of stories I do at your suggestion versus the proportion that are my idea. Give me opportunities not only to discover the best part of myself, but to use that part when you make assignments. Talk to me, even if it's only once a year, about what my goals are, for next year and for five years from now.
10. Get off your butt and walk around. Feel the newsroom. Be a part of it, of us, the reporters. Don't be a bureaucrat. Be a leader.

. . . and Ten Things Editors Want from Their Reporters

1. I want you to respond enthusiastically to each assignment, whether it's your idea or mine. I want to know that you will give it your best.

2. I want you to trust me. I want you to see me as someone who cares as much as, or more than, you do about what we're producing. Many things I ask you to do may not directly benefit you, but will have indirect benefits down the line.

3. I want you to meet our agreed-on length and time requirements.

4. I want you to be as appreciative of a good edit as I am of a good reporting and writing job. I want you to appreciate what two brains can do together.

5. I want you to remember that photos matter. I want you to work conscientiously with the photo desk and think visually.

6. I want you to put your heart into the story, to discover not only the factual truth but the emotional truth—what really matters to the readers, to the characters in your story, to our society. I want that hunger every time.

7. I want you to take your job seriously but not personally. I want you to be able to lose without it breaking your heart, whether it's not getting a story on page one, having it held a day, or having the lead changed by someone above us. I want you to understand that nobody wins 'em all, that tomorrow is another opportunity, that there are no "enemies" in the newsroom.

8. Realize that I respect and appreciate your need to share, but I am burdened by several other reporters and other administrative demands. Don't take it personally if I seem distracted sometimes

9. If I suggest a rewrite and you don't like it, I want you to articulate your position forcefully, but I also expect you to be able to come up with an alternative rather than simply digging in your heels. Be willing to give another version a try. I'm willing to listen; I may even learn something.

10. I want you to be aggressive, creative, resourceful, audacious, dramatic—even if you tried being all those things yesterday and it didn't work. If the *Times* is only as good as our readers expect it to be, it's a failure. We have to transcend their expectations. We have to astonish and delight and amaze and surprise and dazzle them in our explanations of how the world works.

BIBLIOGRAPHY

Resources used to develop this book include:

Bandler, Richard, and Grindler, John. *The Structure of Magic I.* Palo Alto, Calif.: Science & Behavior Books, 1975.

Bronowski, Jacob. *The Ascent of Man.* (Boston: Little, Brown, 1973).

Bryan, W. L., and Harter, N. "Studies in Telegraphic Language" and "Studies in the Physiology and Psychology of the Telegraphic Language." *Psychological Review,* Vol. 4 and 6 (1897).

Buzan, Tony. *Use Both Sides of Your Brain.* New York: E. P. Dutton, 1976.

Calder, Nigel. *The Mind of Man.* London: British Broadcasting Co., 1970.

Cooper, Cary, and Payne, Roy. *Stress at Work.* New York: John Wiley and Sons, 1978.

"Creativity, Management and the Minds of Man." *Human Resource Management,* Spring 1973.

Dimond, Stewart. *The Double Brain.* Edinburgh: Churchill Livingstone, 1972.

Edwards, Betty. *Drawing on the Right Side of the Brain.* Los Angeles: J. P. Tarcher, 1979.

Ferguson, Marilyn. *The Brain Revolution.* New York: Taplinger, 1973.

Gazzaniga, Michael S. "The Split Brain in Man." *Scientific American,* August 1967.

Geschwind, Norma. "Language and the Brain." *Scientific American,* April 1972.

Halacy, Daniel S. *Man and Memory.* New York: Harper & Row, 1970.

Harper, Robert J. *The Cognitive Process: Readings.* Englewood Cliffs, N.J.: Prentice-Hall, 1964.

John, E. Roy. "How the Brain Works—A New Theory." *Psychology Today,* May 1976.

Jones, D. Stanley. *Kibernetics of Mind and Brain.* Springfield, Ill.: Charles C. Thomas, 1970.

Klatzky, Roberta. *Human Memory: Structure and Processes.* San Francisco: W. H. Freeman & Co., 1975.

Levine, Seymour. "Stress and Behavior." *Scientific American,* January 1971.

Luria, A. R. *The Working Brain.* New York: Basic Books, 1973.

McGuigan, F. J., and Schoonover, R. A. *The Psychophysiology of Thinking.* New York: Academic Press, 1973.

McLean, Alan A. *Occupational Stress.* Springfield, Ill.: Charles C. Thomas, 1974.

Michener, James A. *Sports in America.* New York: Random House, 1976.

Pribham, Karl E. "The Neurophysiology of Remembering." *Scientific American,* January 1969.

Rosner, Stanley, and Abt, Lawrence. *The Creative Experience.* New York: Grossman, 1970.

Russell, Bertrand. *The ABC of Relativity.* London: George Allen & Unwin, 1925.

Schlesinger, Benno. *Higher Cerebral Functions and Their Clinical Disorders.* New York: Grune & Stratton, 1962.

Selye, Hans. *Stress in Health and Disease.* Boston: Butterworths, 1976.

Suojanen, Waino W. "Addiction and the Minds of Man." Third Annual Southeast Drug Education Conference, May 1977.

Triesman, Anne. "The Effect of Irrelevant Material on the Efficiency of Selective Listening." *American Journal of Psychology,* December 1964.

Welford, A. T. *Skilled Performance: Perceptual and Motor Skills.* Glenview, Ill.: Scott, Foresman, 1976.

Welford, A. T., and Houssiadas, L. *Contemporary Problems in Perception.* London: Taylor & Francis, 1970.

Wilson, Edward O. "Animal Communication." *Scientific American,* 1976.

Credits

Page 48   From E. Yellin, "A Changing South Revisits Its Unsolved Racial Killings." *New York Times*, 8 November 1999. Reprinted by permission.

Page 110   From E. Goode, "Gentle Drive to Make Voters of Those with Mental Illness." *New York Times*, 13 October 1999. Reprinted by permission.

Page 111   From Rebecca Blumenstein and Joann S. Lublin, "Ante Up! Big Gambles in the New Economy." *The Wall Street Journal*, 2 November 1999, A-1. Reprinted by permission.

Page 112 (top)   From David Wessel, "When It Came Down, the Vile Berlin Wall All But Disappeared." *The Wall Street Journal*, 21 September 1999, A-1. Reprinted by permission.

Page 112 (bottom)   From Peter Waldman, "Silicon Valley, Where the Conversation Comes with a Caveat." *The Wall Street Journal*, 3 November 1999, A-1. Reprinted by permission.

Page 113   From Rebecca Quick, "True Grit, or How Sights Denim Makes Money in Dirty Jeans." *The Wall Street Journal*, 12 October 1999, A-1. Reprinted by permission.

Page 131 (top)   From Howe Berhovek, "National Guard Is Called to Quell Trade-Talk Protests; Seattle Is under Curfew after Disruptions." *New York Times*, 1 December 1999. Reprinted by permission.

Page 131 (bottom)   Reprinted by permission of Associated Press.

Page 143 (bottom)   Copyright 1998, USA Today. Reprinted with permission.

Page 164   From W. Stevens, "Drought May Have Doomed the Lost Colony." *New York Times*, 24 April 1998. Reprinted by permission.

Extracts appearing throughout the Appendix are from the L.A. Times publication "Nuts and Bolts" and are used by permission of the authors.